Tom Sa

A Modern-Day Mess~~...~~

"It is a privilege to take an inside look at one of the most unique prophets of our time. Chesbro's personal, long-time friendship with Tom Sawyer offers a glimpse into the mind and supernatural abilities of this Christ-like individual. The life and times of a modern-day saint is a spiritual journey for the reader. Whether it's bilocation, meditating on the Ganges River, or healing a terminal patient, Tom truly was a gift from God. The reader will travel into another dimension of time and space via the amazing adventures of Tom Sawyer and Dan Chesbro."

—**Mary Grace,** parapsychologist, spiritual teacher, and author of *The Communion of Saints*

"Over the past decade I have had the privilege of sitting at the feet of Rev. Chesbro as he would teach us and tell us the inspiring stories about the wonderful first-hand experiences he had witnessed with Tom Sawyer. I am so happy that he has finally put together this book of more than 160 true stories to enlighten and to inspire anyone who reads them. I highly recommend them to you! This is a book about modern-day miracles."

—**Rev. Gary Nobuo Niki**, coach and consultant in energy healing modalities, Shamanic Samurai Medicine Man, and author of *D.I.Y. ZEN and the Art of Gentle Emotional Transformation*

"This book is a great gift to humanity. Those who read it will learn the power of choosing 'love and creativity against a backdrop of greed and ego.' These stories about Tom Sawyer can open a path to increased hope, healing, peace, prosperity, and joy at this time in the world. I hope you will feel as blessed reading it as I did."

—**Rev. Marta D. Ockuly, Ph.D.,** humanistic psychologist, educator, researcher, and CEO of Creative Potential Institute

"Rev. Chesbro and Rev. Erickson have collaborated to present a compelling and easy-to-read narrative of what one person did to positively affect so many others and even the entire world. I found myself drawn in and continually delighted to learn how Thomas Joseph Sawyer was tuned in to the contract he had on Earth with the Creator and how he followed the guidance that he intuited. Sawyer demonstrated that death doesn't exist, prevented nuclear war on numerous occasions, and served as a bridge between the Age of Pisces and the Age of Aquarius. This exploration of the life of Thomas Joseph Sawyer is among the best."

—**Jerry J. Wellik, Ed.D.,** professor emeritus of special education and master healer of Ericksonian hypnosis

Tom Sawyer
A Modern-Day
Messenger from God

His Extraordinary Life and
Near-Death Experiences

REV. DANIEL CHESBRO
with Rev. James B. Erickson

 FINDHORN PRESS

Findhorn Press
One Park Street
Rochester, Vermont 05767
www.findhornpress.com

Text stock is SFI certified

Findhorn Press is a division of Inner Traditions International

---

Disclaimer
The information in this book is given in good faith and intended for information only. Neither authors nor publisher can be held liable by any person for any loss or damage whatsoever which may arise directly or indirectly from the use of this book or any of the information therein.

Cataloging-in-Publication data for this title is available from the Library of Congress

ISBN 978-1-64411-516-9 (print)
ISBN 978-1-64411-517-6 (ebook)

Printed and bound in the United States by Lake Book Manufacturing Inc. The text stock is SFI certified. The Sustainable Forestry Initiative® program promotes sustainable forest management.

10 9 8 7 6 5 4 3 2 1

Edited by Nicky Leach
Cover photo by Dreamstime.com (ID 27533578 © 2day929)
Text design and layout by Richard Crookes
This book was typeset in Adobe Garamond Pro

To send correspondence to the authors of this book, mail a first-class letter to the authors c/o Inner Traditions • Bear & Company, One Park Street, Rochester, VT 05767, USA and we will forward the communication, or contact the author directly at **http://goldenlionmedia.com/sotb**.

To Maryanne and Joey Yannacone,
who provided years of love, support,
and a space at "Pal Joey's Salon"
for Tom Sawyer's teachings.

Hundreds of people benefitted
from this Love Gesture.

For nothing will be impossible with God.

~ Luke 1:37

Truly, truly, I say to you,

Whoever believes in me,

the works that I do will he do also;

and greater works than these will he do . . .

~ John 14:12

Contents

Foreword

I am grateful to my dear friend, Rev. Dan Chesbro, for giving me this opportunity to write a foreword for this treasure trove of short stories about the life and times of Thomas Joseph Sawyer (Tom Sawyer). Tom is known for having had an extraordinary death experience, and his exceptional story of being crushed under his truck and coming back to life after having been dead for 15 minutes has been captured in other must-read books. But this book of short stories is special for different reasons, because it gives a glimpse into some of the little-known, yet miraculous and awe-inspiring events and occurrences that were part of the ordinary, day-to-day activities and involvements of Tom Sawyer.

There is no better person than Rev. Dan Chesbro to put these memories of Tom to paper. Dan and Tom shared a bond of timeless, deep friendship, and they shared a mission, too—that of facilitating the emergence of the Ancient Order of Melchizedek in our times to assist in the birthing of a new era for humanity, Earth, and all sentient beings. Dan Chesbro has written about how the Order of Melchizedek came into being for these times in his book, *The Order of Melchizedek: Love, Willing Service, and Fulfillment* (Findhorn Press 2010).

I first met Tom Sawyer in the summer of 1988, when I traveled from Ottawa, Canada, to Geneseo, New York, to attend the Sanctuary of the Beloved's Visions of Tomorrow Annual Conference. I had heard that a person named Dan Chesbro was performing ordinations into the Great White Brotherhood (Family of Light). I first learned about the ancient teachings of the Great White Brotherhood in the 1970s, when I lived for several years as a member of the now well-known spiritual community of Findhorn in northern Scotland. And just as I had felt an unmistakable and irresistible pull to go to Findhorn in 1975, I felt the very same strong soul-calling to travel to meet Dan Chesbro and be ordained.

Thus began many years of a deep and abiding connection with the Order of Melchizedek, and a strengthening of my participation in the Family of Light that had begun at Findhorn 13 years previously. Unbeknownst to me at the time was the fact that the energy of Findhorn itself had a role in the creation of what was to become the ordination ceremony for the Order of Melchizedek.

There was a buzz among the participants at the conference that first year I attended, in 1988, and in every subsequent year I attended; the excitement was about this man called Tom Sawyer. Tom already had a following of local students, priests in the Order of Melchizedek, and they were eager to learn from the infinite storehouse of knowledge that Tom brought back from his death experience in 1978. You see, Tom had completely blended with that Light and Love that is Total Knowledge. So a small group of friends met weekly with Tom, and many of the stories in this book reflect Dan Chesbro's memories of those meetings.

Tom could answer questions on any topic, from physics to Earth changes, the true story of the life of Jesus, to future possibilities and probabilities for humankind. All one had to do was ask. Tom considered it extremely important to answer each question as thoroughly and completely as possible. Thus, at the conferences, when Tom arrived on a summer's night, the word would quickly spread that "Tom's here!" and conference participants would settle into an all-nighter, listening to Tom talk and answer questions into the wee hours of the morning. In appreciation of his diligence, someone had t-shirts made up that fondly and humorously said, "I spent the night with Tom Sawyer."

Here was a man who, by all outward appearances, lived an ordinary life. Tom's day job was heavy-duty equipment operator for the City of Rochester, and he was married and the father of two children. And yet, he was always on call to God. He traveled and did things always "on purpose," being at the right place at the right time with the right person or group of people to be of service in large and small ways. He made a huge difference in the lives of many, many people. His exceptional gifts of knowing and knowledge were coupled with his incredible physical strength—a strength that was enhanced from his years of training as an Olympic athlete. Tom radiated great Love, and I always will remember his ever-present humor and delight with just being with us at the conferences.

Tom accomplished extraordinary things in his life. He fulfilled three very important assignments that came back with him from his death experience:

1. Teach that death does not exist.

2. Prevent a nuclear war from beginning in the Middle East in the summer of 1988.

3. Facilitate the ancient Order of Melchizedek.

In fulfilling these objectives he changed the world for all humanity.

Tom carried out these assignments and so much more out of the glare of publicity. Yes, he was a guest on the Oprah and Phil Donahue shows, where he was invited to share his death experience, but he never drew public attention to his activities after his death experience, knowing that he could accomplish more out of the glare of the media spotlight.

The magic and wonder of Tom's life and work has not been written about until now. And there are hundreds more unusual and miraculous stories out there that are yet to be shared by those who met Tom briefly, or who were his friends, colleagues, or acquaintances. If you have stories to share, please let us know, so that the world can know of this extraordinary Messenger of God, who served the human condition that all might benefit from his personal experience of God/Love.

If you are reading about Thomas Joseph Sawyer here for the first time, I invite you to suspend all preconceived beliefs about what is possible for any human being to do.

In closing I would like to express my deep respect and appreciation for Rev. Dan Chesbro, who, in compiling these brief stories of Tom, has provided readers with a glimpse into the extraordinary person that Tom was, making visible for those with eyes to see and a heart to know, the great gift that Tom was to our world. He was a Messenger of God. Tom taught us that death does not exist in the Universe, he prevented nuclear wars on several occasions, and he promoted the Order of Melchizedek. Tom taught us that there is only God, and there is only Good beyond our imaginings. Bless you, Dan, and bless you, Tom.

~ Rev. Sandy Stewart, MSW
Ottawa, Canada

A Challenge

Rev. Tammy Eckert is a Melchizedek priest who, as part of her service, volunteered to record and transcribe this collection of stories to facilitate their being brought to everyone's attention through the publication of this book. She gained much from her experience and would like you, the reader, to benefit as well, so she offers you the following challenge.

Every story in this book is extraordinary. Reading it can allow you to become an integral part of each. This is what this book offers. The energetic life force written in each word is felt, infused, and, if you allow it, brings to you, the reader, a knowing of the truth of Tom Sawyer and of God.

What a glorious moment in "time" this is. Tom Sawyer, a Christed Being, one who was at-One-ment with God, walked with us in this "time." As a result, my life, my understanding of the life I have chosen, is much clearer for what I have come to know during my work with Rev. Dan Chesbro and Tom Sawyer. I have recalled so much from many lifetimes, and that each lifetime I knew, as I do now, that I am loved, protected, and "on purpose."

My challenge questions for you are: Can you allow yourself to be open to this opportunity of knowing God—Total Knowledge—the Unconditional Love that abounds everywhere? What would it take for you to know that you are loved beyond the beyond?

It has been my honor to work with Rev. Dan Chesbro bringing to life this compilation of true stories. I am humbled to have been asked, joyous to know that I know, and grateful beyond words for the teachings of Tom Sawyer and Rev. Dan Chesbro.

~ Rev. Tammy Eckert

Introduction

Among humans, storytelling is universal. It is what connects us to our humanity, links us to our history, and gives us a peek at our possible futures. It automatically appears during childhood, and, as far as I know, can be found in every culture on the planet. Additionally, it goes back in history as far as anyone knows—I have heard that the elements of some stories go back 6,000 years. It is so pervasive that it is taken to be a human adaptation for creating, cementing, and maintaining social bonds while promoting cooperation among individuals and groups.

I understand that in some societies, storytelling has a value that well exceeds what you might expect; that both storytelling and the storytellers themselves are more highly prized than basic skills such as hunting, fishing, foraging, and medical knowledge. At first glance this seems quite odd, as those skills are conducive to survival. But historically, and especially among indigenous populations, stories typically have a content that encourages cooperation, egalitarianism, and gender equality, and these are higher-order survival skills that lead to social cohesiveness, order, and survival of the group. Understand this, and the value placed on this aspect of culture begins to make a lot more sense. And there's more. It has been found that in some of these societies, storytellers have more children, and the best storytellers are considered the prime choice for a living companion.

This really should not be surprising, for storytelling typically reinforces the ethics, norms, mores, and sanctions of the culture. Storytelling is one way we both shape our existence and make sense of it; a way to make sense out of the chaos of human existence. This is all to say, that accomplished storytellers are the keepers of valuable cultural knowledge, and they are responsible for passing this knowledge intergenerationally.

It seems that we need stories and use them for very cogent reasons. Stories enable us to feel things we haven't felt so we can experience pain, joy, heartache, love, and so forth, thereby gaining empathy. Similarly, stories allow us to reexperience those feelings we have in common with others, thereby reaffirming our own humanity and reinforcing that we are not alone in those respects. In addition, in stories, we may see ourselves in such a way as to gain insight and understanding into who and what we are, and perhaps who and what we'd like to become, and become motivated to change, develop, and grow.

In stories, we can find friends in the characters we'd like to have as friends and love in the characters we are attracted to, aiding in sharpening our criteria for selecting such people in life. In addition, a tale containing caveats for outcomes that are less than desirable can serve as cautions for behavior, especially in social interaction.

Stories entertain, teach, educate, entice, provoke, agitate, incite, intellectually stimulate, inspire, predict, shape social thinking and action, dispel ignorance, promote tolerance and compassion, model social justice, express beauty, and often show us our reflection, however hard it may be to look at.

However, the process of storytelling is a two-way street. Over time, storytellers have learned that their audiences prefer stories with a beginning, a middle, and an end. Furthermore, audiences are drawn to stories that contain characters like themselves, or at least have characteristics they can relate to. In addition, audiences like to be drawn into the story, and to use their imaginations to participate in the action. So the best storytellers use every tool at their disposal: tone, tempo, timbre, volume, rhythm, breathing pattern, facial expression, eye movements, body movement, proxemics, gestures, and so forth, to enrich the imagination of their listeners, and hence, their experience of the story. This makes the building of a climax, coupled with a satisfying ending, all the more enjoyable.

The society we now live in could not exist without the gifts of generations past. Human beings are creatures of habit, and we hand down knowledge (and its lessons) from one generation to the next. We want to take pride in leaving a body of knowledge for our descendants to utilize to avoid our mistakes and the mistakes of the past, while continuing our rich cultural traditions and improving the human condition. We hope to give our descendants insights into the problems we've faced and an advantage not found in other species: a pool of communal knowledge. Storytelling enables this movement of knowledge; therefore, it is my belief that story-telling is the single most important tradition humans engage in.

What follows is a collection of stories about actual events that took place between 1978 and 2007. No, they are not very historic; however, the teachings, lessons, insights, and understanding they provide are timeless. They are what one may call "extra-cultural," in that they deal with aspects of the culture, both past and present, and the culture's relationship with Deity and individual relationships.

May you see some of yourself in these accounts, and recognize characteristics you share with those involved, firing your imagination and being drawn in to participate, thereby creating your own action. Enjoy the experience and enjoy yourself, remembering you are loved.

~ **Rev. James B. Erickson**

In the Beginning

The First Meeting

There is a Reader's Digest exercise that asks you to write a story about the most influential person you've ever met. I would like to share some true stories with you about an incredible friend of mine. What this man embodied was (and is) divine. What he did with the life he had was extraordinary. The fellow's name was Tom Sawyer.

This is not Mark Twain's character Tom Sawyer, Huck Finn's friend; this is an actual person who was born in upstate New York. His full name was Thomas Joseph Sawyer, an interesting name when you discover its meaning. The name Thomas is from the Greek word *Didymus* and means "the twin"; the name Joseph means "and God will add"; and a sawyer is a carpenter or a twig in a stream or river, which changes the course of the river forever. Tom fulfilled all those functions in his lifetime: he was a carpenter; he changed the course of human history; and he was a twin of the Essence of God.

As Thomas, he was and is a twin soul of the Light, functioning as a divine messenger to Earth and the human condition. Tom, having been homogenized in the Light of Total Knowledge, which is Unconditional Love, became an Ambassador of the Almighty, or a Messenger of God.

As Joseph ("God will add"), the human Tom Sawyer was spiritually enhanced by God and raised into enlightenment and total compassion. The contract between God and Tom called for Tom's death and resurrection in the 20th and 21st centuries.

As a sawyer—that is, one who saws or is a carpenter—Tom excelled: he was a fine carpenter, indeed. For the second meaning, Tom's contract called for him to change the course of the river of humanity by standing in the stream of consciousness. The result is that everything has been changed, and changed for the positive. He came back from the dead to prevent nuclear disasters and the assassination of the Dalai Lama and to foster new understanding about the nature of God and the workings of the Universe.

It was in the month of February when I met Tom for the first time. I was giving a lecture in Rochester, New York, at a Unity Church. Off to my right was a man sitting on the edge of his seat and intently listening to everything I had to say—I became very aware of him being there. Later that evening, he came and asked me a question or two, but I can't recall what the questions were.

It was shortly after that that the manager of my TV program, The Open Door, a spiritually based talk show, asked me if I would like to know who my guest was going to be for the coming week. She said the guest was Tom Sawyer.

I laughed and said, "Becky Thatcher and Huckleberry Finn?"

But she made a reference to Raymond Moody's book, *Life after Life*, saying, "Tom's story is like that. It's about his death experience. I think it will make a good show."

For the show with Tom, I drove from my farm to the studio. There had been a snowstorm, and I had rocked my car back and forth to get out of my driveway. I broke the fan belt but didn't know that was the case, so I proceeded to drive the 40 minutes to the studio. I arrived pretty much on time, and the car died. I met Tom, and he seemed nothing out of the ordinary. The stage crew and I did some camera and sound tests as Tom sat patiently, dressed in his blue sweater. I realized later that he always wore blue, as the color was reminiscent of being in the Light during his death experience.

Ordinarily, the show would have been taped in an hour and then shown during the course of the week, but as Tom retold the story of his death experience, every time he started talking about the Light, he would weep with the sheer joy of the memory of that experience and we would have to stop filming and begin again. We did the interview, and he explained the accident he had had. As he talked, I was visualizing what he was saying, and it was like watching a movie. (I was made aware later that he knew how I was thinking at that time.)

When we took a break, someone asked him a question, and he responded by talking about a little girl called Sarapha. Sarapha's mother was Jewish, and her father was a Roman soldier; therefore, she was an outcast from both the Jewish people and the Romans and ended up working at the inn where Jesus was to be born. It had been arranged that Mary and Joseph would stay at the inn, which was operated by Essenes. But Bethlehem was so chaotic, as was the inn, the innkeeper and his wife said that there was no suitable place for a newborn there, and instead, they were sent out to the grotto, which served as a stable.

Tom explained that before Sarapha's birth, she had asked God if she could be present when baby Jesus was born. The innkeepers had Sarapha bring the swaddling clothes for the baby, and she was present when the baby was born. Tom said that when Sarapha brought the linen and held the baby, it was the peak experience that fulfilled her life then and there. The rest of her life was full of turmoil, but she always had the memory of the experience of holding Jesus's infant body. That memory sustained her for the rest of her life—this spiritual encounter with Deity. It was interesting for me to hear this story, since I had just recently read Edgar Cayce's account of Sarapha's life. After Tom related this story, we went back into production and finished the taping.

Looking back now, I am aware that Tom knew of my having just read Edgar Cayce's story about Sarapha. It was his way of making a deeper connection with me and showing me that there was more here than simply someone talking about their death experience. It was the very first example of Tom demonstrating to me his access to extraordinary knowledge. At that time, I didn't know that when he had died he had had access to Total Knowledge, but he knew everything about Edgar Cayce's life and all of his readings.

Later, when we were going for lunch, I got into my car and found that the battery was dead, so I went with Tom in his car. He made an interesting side comment, saying, "Prior to my death experience I probably would have spit on a gay person—not now." He wanted me to know that he was perfectly okay with who and what I am. I was not out as a gay person at that time, but Tom could see me totally for who I am, even though he had only just met me. He loved me unconditionally, as God does.

We went off to the auto parts store to get a fan belt, which he was going to install, because he was a master mechanic. Tom managed to get the wrong part, but in retrospect I realize that his "error" enabled us to have one full day together. In the years that followed, and over the course of our history together, we spent very few full days together.

On our way to lunch, we came upon a bus that was stuck in a snow bank. He got out of his car and went behind the bus to push it out. I sat in the passenger side watching him do this, not thinking it was anything unusual. Later he would tell this story, saying that I helped with the bus, but in my reality, I never got out of the car.

We later had lunch at the home of a crew member from the show. During lunch, the hostess was asking Tom questions, and one of the questions was, "Why did all the dinosaurs disappear on the earth?" Tom responded, "God caused a vapor to come around the Earth, and within 36 hours the dinosaurs were gone." Tom also intimated that a meteor hit the earth, and that caused the vapor. Of course, we now know this to be true. There were many other questions, including questions about Jesus Christ, but unfortunately, I don't recall the answers.

It was the evening of the first day that we met, and the master mechanic Tom had managed to get an improper fan belt. Once he got the right one and installed it in my car, we sat in his car talking, and he said to me, "You know, certain people have been chosen to do certain things," implying that either he or I were designated to do certain things for God. I didn't know him that well, and I thought, Oh, my God, maybe he's a megalomaniac! At that time, I had no idea of the work he was to do and the capabilities he had. When I was driving home, I realized that I had met a really interesting character, but I had no recognition of the many years we'd work together and what all the results would be.

Tom Sawyer Died May 23, 1978

The following information is what Tom shared with us about his death experience during the taping of the program. I share this with you now because you need to grasp this to understand him. I precede it with this information: Tom's birth date was September 9, 1945. He was born on the 9th day of the 9th month, at the 9th hour, the 9th minute, and the 9th second—to infinity. In numerology, this is the vibration of a redeemer or a high spiritual teacher.

It was early in the evening of May 23, 1978, and Tom was in his garage. He had his pickup truck up on jack stands and 4x4s and was showing his very young sons how to fix a transmission. The pickup truck was filled with firewood, so it was very heavy. Unbeknownst to Tom, there was an air pocket under the driveway from when the house had been constructed

13 years before. Due to that air pocket and the weight of the truck, the jacks punched through the driveway, and the truck collapsed on him. When the truck fell on him, the weight of it crushed his chest and a bolt pierced his side. Tom held his breath as long as he could, while his eyes were almost popping out of his skull from the pressure on his chest, then he blacked out and stopped breathing. Tom had trained as an Olympic athlete, and he was physically fit, but he was no match for the weight of the truck. There were jack stands nearby that could have been used to extricate him, but in the chaos of the situation no one noticed them.

On the day of his death he was about five months shy of his 33rd birthday. It is interesting to note that other great spiritual teachers, such as Sai Baba and Jesus Christ, either began or finished their work at age 33. Multiples of the number 11 are considered master numbers, and there are major and minor solar flares from our sun every 11 and 22 years.

At this point in his life, Tom's belief system did not include God, and he thought that Jesus Christ was a fairytale, so he had an awakening on many levels.

As Tom lost consciousness, everything appeared to be a bombardment of millions of colors of light, opalescence, and phosphorescence—colors that we cannot see with the human eye. First, Tom experienced the blackness, the void. This blackness was not a void as we think of a void; that is, empty. It was the exact opposite: a tremendous fullness—the fullness of God; the potential of God becoming; the same void mentioned in the beginning in Genesis.

Tom would later recall that he felt totally awake, like a fully awakened being, at that moment, and that there was Love in that experience—total Unconditional Love. Then Tom realized that there is only God and only Good. That was his first experience of God—the moment of being in the blackness, the void, the Great No-Thing. There appeared to be a tunnel and, at infinity, a point of Light that he recognized as God. Then he realized that the void was God; the tunnel was God; the point of Light at the end of the tunnel was God; that all of it was an experience of God.

Tom began to accelerate through the tunnel at the speed of Light, which is what Love does, toward the origin of the Light, and as he went his life review began. A life review is a reexperiencing of everything that one has experienced at the subjective, objective, and spiritual levels of this life—all simultaneously. You not only experience your life review from your memories but from the memories of everyone you have had any interaction with. For example, if you slapped someone, you will feel the impact of the slap as if you were the recipient, and what happened to that person as a result of that slap. You are not responsible for what someone else chooses to feel or do because of what you did, but you become aware of the domino effect of their choice(s) as a result of your interaction with them and the results of your choices.

For example, in his life review Tom reexperienced the time when, in his youth, he was driving his truck down Lake Avenue in Rochester. He had just recently put four brand new tires on his truck, and he was quite proud of it. An elderly man suddenly appeared before him, and he had to slam on his brakes to avoid hitting him. This really angered Tom because, from his point of view, his tires were wrecked from having to brake so suddenly. To make matters worse, the old man walked around the driver's side of the truck to the open window, reached in, and slapped Tom across the face, calling him "a young whippersnapper." Tom flew into a rage, jumped out of his truck, and punched the old man in the face 32 times before the man fell to the pavement and hit his head. If Tom had hit him any harder on his nose, he would have driven the bone into the man's brain and killed him. (Tom reacted irrationally and violently because his father had taught him to protect himself in such a manner.) Tom then drove off, leaving the old man in the street.

In his life review, Tom reexperienced all that he did to this elderly gentleman. He knew who the man was, his name, his age, that his wife had died earlier, and that was when he had begun to drink. The man had just left "his" stool in his favorite bar. He was inebriated and was trying to find his way home when he staggered into the street and was startled by a young man in a truck. He felt perfectly justified walking around the side of the truck and reaching in through the open window and slapping the young man in the face, just as Tom had felt totally justified in hitting him 32 times. They both felt justified.

Then Tom experienced being the old man, and experienced himself punching himself in his face 32 times. In a life review, you will be the person you raped, as well as the rapist. You will experience all facets of the event from every perspective and from every viewpoint. And even so, God will only love you unconditionally.

There was a woman and her husband who witnessed Tom beating the elderly gentleman. In his life review, Tom experienced how it had affected her. It had rekindled her childhood memories and emotional trauma of being beaten. Tom experienced her turmoil as well. He experienced everything impinging on that scene—the temperature of the sky, the plane flying overhead, the people in the plane and their first names. He even became aware that there were paint cans under a sign on top of a building a block or so away. (Years later he went to the top of that building, and the paint cans were still there, just as they were during his life review.)

Everything you ever experienced from the instant of your conception to the moment of your death you reexperience. This includes all the dreams you have ever had, but now you will know what your dreams meant and what your soul was teaching you. Tom later said it would take 10 years of talking nonstop to do adequate justice to his life review.

Tom continued down the tunnel to the origin, to the point of Light. One of the lovely life-review stories from Tom was when he was a young boy walking in the woods. He was nine or 10 years old and he was admiring the trees and having fun walking in the woods. It was autumn, and he came across a beautiful maple tree in its gorgeous autumn splendor. Tom thought, "What a beautiful tree!" In his life review, he learned that the tree was observing him and thinking, "What a cute little child."

There were 33 years of accumulated life experience that Tom reviewed in this way, and it was complete in an instant. Then he reached the point of Origin. He had never seen anything as beautiful as that Light, and God asked him if he had any questions. Tom had 13 questions, and most of them were of a personal nature, but one of them was about Jesus (which, at that time, Tom thought was a fairytale). He asked if Jesus was real, and did he really live in a town called Nazareth? Tom said that instantly it was as if he was a speck of dust on Jesus's shoulder looking backward in time. He could see all the past lives of Jesus, including His past life as Melchizedek.

It is all quite real.

Tom had agreed to die and come back at 33 years of age, as it was necessary to intercede for the human condition. In the Light, God said that if he, Tom, wanted to fulfill his contract he would have to step forward, or incline toward the event. God could not interfere with Tom's free will. Tom would then be dead; he would have given up his free will; and he would not be able to return to "normalcy" in the human condition.

Tom reported, "I don't remember whether I said yes, or inclined toward the contract, but I merged and became part of Total Knowledge."

Total Knowledge is Unconditional Love and equals Compassion.

There were three things that Tom was asked to do:

1. Teach that death doesn't exist.

2. Prevent nuclear war (summer of 1988).

3. Assist in bringing the Order of Melchizedek into the Age of Aquarius.

When Tom stepped forward, he merged and became part of Total Knowledge; he became aware of all history and of the present moment everywhere and all probable futures.

When he was in Total Knowledge, he saw the life review of Edgar Cayce. He said that when Cayce died, he was on his knees praying about his obsession with things in his personal life. In Tom's life review, he experienced all the readings Edgar had given. Tom said that everything Edgar Cayce talked about in his readings was 100 percent accurate, and that it was exactly what Tom had seen when he became part of Total Knowledge. Tom also experienced the lives of Albert Einstein, Max Plank, and Neils Bohr (just to name a few), and he knew them intimately and personally. When he returned to life on planet Earth, he was greatly disappointed to discover that they had all passed, for he thought he could walk down the street and have a cup of coffee with them, so to speak.

For example, he knew that Einstein had passed, leaving behind information used to create a nuclear weapon, and of the anxiety that Albert took with him because of that. Later, Tom sent a message to Albert's sister that her brother was now at peace because there was no more concern about nuclear war at that point.

Spiritually, Tom then came back down the tunnel to his body, which was still pinned beneath the truck. He experienced the tunnel as a mathematical formula. He didn't have a near-death experience—he died and came back; he was a reincarnated being within his incarnation. However, what returned to his body was a tremendously spiritually enhanced being. Since he had become one with Total Knowledge, God, when he came back, he was more of God and less of Tom. For example, and among other things, he now had the ability to multilocate.

In his multiple-locations state, he witnessed the state trooper who was on his way to assist Tom while he was pinned under the truck, and knew all that the trooper was thinking, all of his concerns, such as meeting Tom's wife in her distress and getting home late for supper (again) and how his own wife would feel about that. At the same time, Tom was also with the two paramedics who were in the ambulance driving to the scene. They knew Tom, and were making comments and asking questions such as, "Now what's he done?"

Tom's next-door neighbor, a Vietnam veteran, had lost his best friend during the war. His friend had bled to death in his arms, and the neighbor had vowed never to have any more buddies like that. Then he moved in next door to Tom. Tom was more like Huckleberry Finn than Tom Sawyer—he rode a motorcycle; he was a carpenter; and he was a man's man—and they had formed a solid relationship.

The neighbor came running out of his house to see what had happened and was told that Tom was dead under the truck. He ran over, knelt down beside Tom, and in his great sorrow and anger said, "You miserable son of a bitch!" and punched him in the head. Tom later joked that the timing was perfect because the jolt helped him come back into his body.

The ambulance, paramedics, and state trooper all arrived, and Tom was finally extricated from beneath the truck. Miraculously (and inexplicably), he was regaining consciousness, and they told him that they needed his permission to take him to the hospital. Basically, Tom said, "No, I'm not going to the hospital.", and then he blacked out again. Because he was unconscious, they could then take him without his permission, but he remained in the hospital for only 12 hours.

After his admission and x-rays, the radiologist came in and said he wanted to meet this man Tom Sawyer. He wanted to keep him and observe him because there was really nothing physically wrong with Tom's body as far as he could tell, but liver or spleen damage was likely.

However, Tom said he was not staying and was going home—and he did! From his death experience, and being in Total Knowledge and having become an enhanced being, Tom knew that there was no reason for him to stay in the hospital, so he got his father-in-law to drive him home. Tom lay on the couch for three days and nights, then he got up and called his mother and said, "Something incredible happened." His wife overheard the conversation. She had just read *Life after Life* by Raymond A. Moody and thought that Tom had had one of those near-death experiences.

Tom Sawyer told me that he would use up three bodies by the time his work was done. And indeed, he had three death experiences during this incarnation. He used his body up in the service of the human condition and fulfilled his contract with God.

Death Does Not Exist

By coming back from the dead Tom Sawyer proved that death does not exist. There were many researchers who spoke with him about his "near" death experience, because that is what they believed he had had. There was a research group from Warner Brothers Motion Pictures, scientists from the University of Connecticut, film crews from France, and all these opportunities to tell about his "near" death experience, which was in fact a death experience. Period.

Albert Einstein theorized that energy cannot be destroyed; it can only change form. Water can become an ice cube and be changed back to water, but the H2O remains, and if not in that form, then perhaps as separate hydrogen and oxygen atoms. Likewise, we are energy when we come into this form, and when we depart we continue as energy.

Stephen Hawking speculated about the existence of neutrinos, then several years later, this invisible energy was discovered in Geneva, Switzerland; Los Alamos, New Mexico, USA; the former Soviet Union; and Sudbury, Ontario, Canada. Scientists tried to capture it in a solution of heavy water to prove its existence. Tom told me that the scientists believed that only 5 percent of the Universe was made up of neutrinos, and that they had not yet realized that it is 100 percent neutrinos.

One of the main things about neutrinos is that they comprise the unified field; this is no longer theory but reality. There isn't anything in creation that isn't made of neutrinos, nothing we can see or not see that isn't made of neutrinos. They don't evolve, but because they exist they allow other things to come into reality. Neutrinos travel faster than the speed of Light, which is what Love does. The most interesting thing about neutrinos is that they have no death cycle, so death doesn't exist in the Universe, for we are literally made of those energies—all parts of the Universe are.

Tom went to Sudbury to meet with scientists and physicists and assist them with their research. He could give them the answers to their equations, but they had to ask. He was not allowed to just give it to them without their asking. So here is a high school graduate teaching some of the greatest scientists of our time, which meant that they had to be open to receiving information from a "lower source." Tom's death experience gave him access to Total Knowledge, and when he talked to the scientists in Sudbury, he asked them why they weren't up on their math.

What the scientists will never find in a laboratory is the nature or makeup of neutrinos, for that makeup is God. It is Unconditional Love; we are living in God's imagination. So nothing experiences death. Change, yes; evolution, yes—there is creation and evolution. But the scientific community hasn't yet told us that they have discovered that death doesn't exist. What they will say is that you cannot destroy energy. The implications are incredibly wonderful, but I don't think that they know how to approach telling us, or even if they have the courage to tell themselves.

When neutrinos were first discovered, Tom and I met for lunch.

I said, "This is great, because it proves that there is no difference between you, a rock, and a hard place, so why can't we have world peace now?"

He said, "Not quite, because this planet is a schoolroom, and we are here to learn about Love and creativity against a backdrop of greed and ego."

Then he asked me, "Do you want to close the school?"

And I replied, "Of course not."

Then he said, "We will have a peaceable kingdom. We will learn how to cohabit with all sentient beings, but there will always be greed and ego. This is a planet of duality."

Many books and films have been made of Tom Sawyer's life experience in which he talks about surviving death, but he is one of very few to experience death who died and came back. I currently don't know of anyone else who had a death experience and merged with Total Knowledge as Tom did. Jesus, who became the Christ, was resurrected from the dead to demonstrate to the human condition that there is no permanent hold on us in death. Still, many make a free-will choice to make all such things a "mystery" for themselves.

The neutrinos that comprise the unified field are no longer theory but reality, and within that reality is the knowledge that death doesn't exist and that the Universe is constantly reincarnating. "Reincarnating" was a term that Tom used, rather than saying "constantly recreating itself," because to reincarnate means to come back into the flesh. The Universe is not a flesh body, but it is constantly reincarnating, while the essence of humans reincarnates also. It is alpha and omega, then alpha again.

Preventing Nuclear Destruction

The first occasion that Tom prevented nuclear disaster came from his awareness of a group called The Sons of God in Lebanon. A suicide bomber from this group had a dirty bomb in a truck and planned to detonate it in Israel. It would have caused a great deal of destruction and death; however, Tom said that even if the terrorists had set off this device in Israel, in 1987, few outside people would have reacted, because of the prejudice and hatred toward the Jewish people.

Tom asked the priests of the Order of Melchizedek to fervently pray to divert this potential action. He gave Tyre, Lebanon, as the place to focus the energy. The suicide bomber was driving to a checkpoint, where he was to detonate the device, and Tom asked the priesthood to pray and send Love to the potential event.

All the Love (Love balming) was focused on the suicide bomber and his target. This resulted in him feeling that Love, and realizing that he could not proceed with the plan. The man said that he felt an incredible Love go through his body, and that he could not complete his mission. Instead, he parked the truck and asked for protection so that he and his family would not be harmed. Once they realized he had aborted his mission, the members of his own group would have killed him and/or his entire family. So at Tom's urging it was Love and prayer that prevented a nuclear event in this instance.

The second prevention of nuclear war was accomplished by Tom calling a friend in Canada, a fellow bike racer from his Olympic days. Tom knew that the United States was going to be testing Tomahawk cruise missiles in Canada, and that a B-52 might potentially crash and cause incredible devastation there, so he made the phone call.

The friend said, "Hell, no! That can't happen!" The friend then contacted some Canadian First Nation people, and they crossed into upstate New York, to the Griffiss Air Force Base in Oneida County, where the B-52s were going to take off. Their protest shut down the project, and the whole program was moved to Nevada, where no one knew of its existence except God, Tom, and the people responsible for the project.

The third time, Tom was working in upstate New York the day they launched the first missile in Nevada. The missile can memorize the surface features of the ground and is used in surgical bombing by traveling just over the surface of the earth and hitting a very specific target. However, if one of the seven computers on board malfunctions, the missile shuts down and crashes and/or is aborted.

Using his ability to multilocate, Tom went out of body and into the missile, into a part of one of the computers, into a molecule in that part, into the atom of a molecule there, to the nucleus of that atom, and waited for an electron to come around in its orbit. He sent unconditional Love to the electron. Everything responds to Love with either a yes or no; nothing is indifferent. The electron shuddered, and that shudder rippled throughout the computer, which created a domino effect through the system and shut down the missile.

Tom did this on three different occasions to three different missiles, and that ended that particular program. Had he not done this, these missiles would eventually have been sold to Saddam Hussein, who had nuclear weapons made available to him, and he would have used them indiscriminately. God and Tom knew that if the missiles were sold to Saddam Hussein, he would have used them and poisoned the world with radiation.

Tom sank three missiles and scuttled the program to prevent nuclear war in the Middle East in the summer of 1988. With the political alliances of the time, there would have been a firebomb reaction encompassing much of the world. As a result, everyone would be poisoned and either dead or dying of cancer today. This "classroom" would have been destroyed.

God will not interfere with human history without our permission. Though God Themself did not interfere in sinking the cruise missiles directly, He/She was able to accomplish that goal by using Tom, with his permission. Tom had given up his free will and had become a messenger from God. Thank God! (There may have been other times when Tom averted nuclear devastation.)

Somebody once asked Tom about the Rapture—the prediction that God would destroy Earth and only the good people would go to Heaven and the rest would go to Hell. Tom said that that interpretation could have been made about nuclear war, but that is not going to happen.

Assisting the Order of Melchizedek

When the age of Pisces began, approximately two thousand years ago, people were praying to Zeus, Jupiter, and Athena (among other gods). Then, in the course of about fifteen hundred years, Buddha, Jesus, and Mohammed appeared and changed the focus of religion. When religion married with politics, women were excluded from power, and doctrine and dogmas were created that resulted in separation among people. Wars ensued. Holocausts were created. It was time to bring back the Priesthood of Melchizedek in its original form, which is replete throughout the entire Universe. The Order of Melchizedek is an eternal order in service, an expression of unconditional Love and service from God. In effect, it is a way that God accomplishes Love to all parts of Themself.

Tom said that when Jesus came to the Earth plane, the Priesthood of Melchizedek was not active, so it became necessary for Him to be sacrificed in order to prove that death doesn't exist, and that God is an unconditional Lover. When Tom began his ministry, the Priesthood of Melchizedek was in the beginning stages and was able to facilitate his work, and he, in turn, was able to assist in its development.

Tom never told me what or how to do this work, but he was always encouraging. One thing he said to me in a dream was, "I especially like it when you read Psalm 110," which says in part: "In the days of your youth, your army will be volunteers. You are now and forevermore a Priest after the Order of Melchizedek."

Since 1986, there have been nearly 17,000 ordinations of people from all around the world. We do not discriminate by age, gender, lifestyle, religion, or in any other way. We have no doctrine nor dogma, no dress code, secret handshake, or club song. Our priests have total freedom. They are in a state of perfection, as God is perfect. Our primary service is toward the human condition; to teach and/or heal during this transition into the Age of Aquarius and toward equality for all sentient beings. This effort is a function of The Law of One. The Law of One is: There is only God, and there is only Good.

Tom attended the priesthood gatherings that were then held every year at Geneseo College in upstate New York. At that time, he would make himself available to teach and to heal, typically for hours, and sometimes he was up the entire night answering all questions thoroughly. He also traveled with the priesthood to Virginia Beach; Sedona, Arizona; Egypt, and Tibet. On his own, he worked for many countries around the world. Tom himself was ordained as a priest on September 15th, 1991, following his second death experience.

Thomas Joseph Sawyer had three death experiences in this incarnation, and he fulfilled his contract with God. The first death experience occurred under a truck in 1978. The second death experience occurred during back surgery in 1990. His third and final death experience occurred on April 28, 2007. He did many things that were supernormal, or divine. These stories relate some of what he did and said.

It is my intent, through this book, to help people become aware of the magnitude of God's Love for us; a Love so completely unconditional and ongoing that He/She continues to send messengers to us. The planet might have been destroyed had Tom Sawyer not agreed to be one of those messengers and fulfill his contract.

The following stories cover a period of over 30 years of Tom's service to the human condition. These true stories will bring you an appreciation of who Thomas Joseph Sawyer was, and is, but more importantly, the magnitude of God's Love for humanity.

Ordinations

This Is Your Job

The following explains why no one else has ever been authorized to perform ordinations into the Order of Melchizedek.

One afternoon, after I had moved to a new office near Lake Ontario, Tom called and asked to come over to see the new arrangement. He came into the office, sat down on my couch, and proceeded to say: "You have sent many people to my house about this question of ordinations, and I want to straighten you out once and for all, and don't send anyone else to my door about this. When I look throughout the entire Universe right now, and I am, you are the only one who has earned the right to do these ordinations, and you are going to do them until the day you die. I don't care if both your arms and legs are broken, no one is to help you with the ceremony. Before you die, you are going to have a dream or vision as to whether you bring this energy back Home with you or pass it on to somebody else. Now that's it, so don't send anyone else to my door asking if they can do ordinations."

Many months later he called me at my home and said: "You know, when I had my life review and had access to Total Knowledge, I saw all of your past lives and future probabilities. This ordination ceremony is your job. If something should happen to you and you die before your time, which, by the way, is not going to happen, I [Tom] would be the only one to do the ordinations. If both you and I died right now, we will have done our work. When I saw your probable future, you are going to live to be an old man, and I don't envy all that you have yet to do."

Ordination Ceremony

On one occasion, I was invited to do ordinations in Montreal, Quebec. There were hundreds of people to be ordained, and they were all dressed in white. It looked like a big confirmation class. I asked some people why everyone was dressed in white, and they told me that they had been instructed to do so. I said, "Oh, there are no rules about dress."

We were there for hours doing ordinations because there were so many people. By the time I finished it was early in the morning, and I was exhausted.

When I came home, I asked Tom if there was any way that I could shorten the ceremony. Tom got back to me later and suggested that I say one prayer that would cover everybody being ordained, instead of the same prayer for each one. He also said that I only need to do the element blessing once. Then he suggested that I put all the crystals in a crystal bowl so that their energies would merge into one, and that way I could use just one crystal.

On Easter Sunday, I put all the crystals in a crystal bowl and placed the bowl out on the kundalini energy path in the back field of my farm. This is a path that has multiple energy areas and resembles a large model of the human spine and chakra centers. That afternoon, the Thunder Beings came with lightning and rain. The next morning, when I went to take the crystals out, I received an electric shock when I touched them.

Tom said that there was nothing more that I could do to shorten ordination, and that the ceremony is magical.

Psalm 110

As noted earlier, I met Tom Sawyer prior to calling the priests into the Order of Melchizedek. He had been a guest on my TV show, The Open Door. After my first meeting with him I had a dream. In the dream, the sky was gray and I was walking through Tom's neighborhood in the town of Greece in upstate New York. In the dream I was naked. I knocked on his door, and Tom's wife opened it and invited me in. Everyone had clothes on but me, but no one seemed to notice or care.

Tom said, "I'm glad you're here, and I'd like you to meet Dan and Carol" (Tom also had friends called Dan and Carol, the same as me and my ex-wife). Tom's wife had baked an angel food cake, and it was sitting on a sideboard with some serving dishes. She asked me if I would like a piece of cake, and I said yes, and held the cake in the appropriate place. His wife said, "I like it when you read scripture, because it sounds like you wrote it."

Then Tom looked at me intently with his clear blue eyes and said, "I especially like it when you read Psalm 110."

I was trying to respond, but all I could come up with was, "I especially like Psalm 95, myself." I could not remember the one I used to quote every Easter Sunday from my pulpit.

He looked at me like I wasn't getting it, and said again, "I especially like it when you read Psalm 110."

When I woke up from the dream, I went to my Bible and looked up Psalm 95, which really didn't have any relevance to what Tom was expressing. Then I read Psalm 110, which begins with: "In the days of your youth, your army will be volunteers. You are now and forevermore a priest after the Order of Melchizedek." Then I went on to find the psalm that I always quoted at Eastertime, Psalm 22. It begins with, "My God, my God, why have you forsaken me?"

Understand that, in Jesus's time, when you quoted the first line, you implied the entire psalm. Psalm 22 goes on to describe the crucifixion and addresses having faith in and praising God. So Jesus, in quoting Psalm 22 from the cross, was not whining or bemoaning that He had been rejected by His Father. Quite the opposite, He was honoring his Father and praising Him: "Let them praise the Lord that seek after Him; may your heart be quickened forever!" (Psalm 22:27)

When it is time to call the priests and perform ordinations, I use Psalm 110 for a part of the ordination ceremony: "You are now and forevermore a priest according to the Order of Melchizedek."

By What Authority?

There were some priests at a weekend conference, and they mentioned to the workshop leader that they had been ordained by Dan Chesbro. The leaders responded by asking, "By what authority does he do this thing?" When I related the story to Tom, he replied, "Gee, I've heard that somewhere before."

The Church Declines to Comment

Father Joseph F. Girzone, a retired Roman Catholic priest, wrote a book entitled *Joshua* (and subsequently several other books using the same character). It is a fictionalized account of what would happen if Jesus came back today, and how he would deal with the Roman Catholic Church. Tom told me that he had read Father Girzone's book, and that except for the very beginning and end it was his (Tom's) story, but that he (Tom) was not Joshua. Years later, it became apparent to me that Tom had taken on the role of a Christed being and Messenger of God. Tom told me that his life was discussed by a council in the Roman Catholic Church, and they had decided to remain silent and avoid drawing attention to him.

What's in a Name?

Tom was baptized and raised a Roman Catholic in a French-Canadian community in the United States. When his mother brought him to be baptized, the Church wanted a first, middle, and last name. His full given name on his birth certificate reads "Thomas Joseph Sawyer," but when his mother spoke to the priest, she insisted that he be baptized "Tom Sawyer." The priest strongly resisted, but Tom's mother said, "You will baptize him Tom Sawyer, or you shall not have him." She was adamant, and so he was baptized "Tom Sawyer." Her reason(s) for doing this are unknown.

When I do ordinations and travel around the world, I mention the name Tom Sawyer, and people smile and their hearts open. They are probably thinking about Becky Thatcher and Huckleberry Finn. Opening their heart chakra and mind makes them willing to listen to the true stories about Tom Sawyer, a Messenger from God, and all that it implies for humanity.

Tom's Ordination

After his second death experience, Tom let me know that it might be necessary for him to be ordained in preparation for the work in Egypt, but, he said, it had to be kept private, with no witnesses. We picked a day, September 15, 1991, and I went to his house and picked him up.

Now, Tom always wore a blue shirt or blue sweater. Blue signified the feminine aspect of God, and he worked with that color. The day I picked him up for his ordination he was wearing a white shirt with black trousers. I was driving around Lake Ontario, looking for a secluded cove or beach, but I didn't know the lake as well as he did. He knew it intimately because of the years of snow-plowing he had done for the city of Greece.

He said, "What you're thinking of is over here," and we went to a secluded cove at Braddock's Bay. I drew a circle in the sand and a five-pointed star, and put a chair down in the middle of the circle facing east. He took his shoes off, and I proceeded to do the ordination ceremony.

At his crown chakra, a bee kept flying around, and I was trying to shoo it away. After I completed the ceremony, he said that the bee had stung him on his left foot, his right foot, and his right calf. He went on to say that when the truck fell on him it had punctured his left side, then, holding up his two hands, he said, "I only need two more."

He started walking toward the lake, and I thought to myself, "Please do not do what I think you are capable of doing, because I will faint right here." He proceeded to walk about half the length of a football field onto Lake Ontario. He stood out on the lake with the water barely up to his ankles in an area that is at least 20 feet in depth. I was standing on the shore in ankle-deep water.

Then he bent over and tasted the water and said, "Oh, it's a good day for Lake Ontario. There are only 18,000 pollutants in the water today." Then he said, "Now Chesbro, don't move. There's a broken Pepsi bottle by your feet, and you can hurt yourself."

I bent down and felt around in the sand, and sure enough, I pulled up a Pepsi bottle with the top broken off. Then he walked toward me, and as he got close, I could see that the only place that was wet on him were the cuffs of his black trousers. One of the priests had given me mala beads, so I took them off and put them around his neck, then we drove back to his house and met our wives. The individuals going on the Tibet and Egypt trip were ordained, and now so was he.

Long ago, the White Brotherhood initiates went to the Great Pyramid for ceremonies. At some point, Tom told me it would have been sacrilegious for him to do the ceremony in the pyramid without having been ordained.

Gold in Your Aura

Tom witnessed his wife's ordination, and afterward talked to me about what happens in the ordination ceremony. He said that one of the results of ordination is that there is more gold in a person's aura, and that gold is an attractor energy. Gold draws to itself, and is providing the priest with greater healing, telepathic, and attracting abilities to gather whatever is needed to accomplish their work. At one point he said to me, "You know, you're playing with fire!"

If an individual has unresolved issues, the energy of the ordination encourages that person to release and let go of their past. Melchizedek priests may become like a little Buddha or Christed being.

Pictures of the White Light

I was in Raleigh, North Carolina, and about two years into performing ordinations. Someone had a camera and was photographing the ceremonies.

When they got the pictures, they said, "There's nothing wrong with the film or camera, but there is a ball of White Light coming into the picture, and it continues, spiraling in, and then it merges with you and the person being ordained."

I was invoking the Light in the ordination ceremony when that picture was taken. When I showed the photos to Tom, he said, "Oh yeah, that Light. I think I've seen that somewhere before."

I show those pictures to new people attending ordination class so they can see what is happening with the spiritual energy during their ordination.

The Holy Grail

When I had my Baptist church, my secretary's mother had a silver chalice. After her mother had graduated (made her transition), my secretary inherited the chalice, and she put it on a pedestal but it kept falling off. Her mother was a Spiritualist, and I believe she was moving the chalice off the pedestal (consider the metaphor).

My secretary gave it to me, saying, "You will probably get more use out of this than I will."

I was very happy to receive it, and that silver chalice has been used for nearly all 17,000 ordinations as of this writing (occasionally, other vessels were, or are, used). It wasn't long after that that my secretary passed and is now with her mother.

The chalice has been around the world twice. One time we were in Tom's kitchen and, in his great sense of humor, he referred to the silver chalice as the Holy Grail. I have always shied away from the idea that the chalice makes the ordination ceremony special in any way. The water it holds is the spiritual quality that contributes to the ceremony. The chalice is covered with silver plate and a lot is worn off. In addition, years ago, my dachshund bit into it and left a couple of dents in it, so it's old and beaten up. Still I take it with me and use it. If it were to disappear we would easily use something else. It reminds me of fond memory of my former secretary and her Spiritualist mother.

The Old Monastery

In the hills in Conesus, there was an abandoned monastery. In bygone days, Catholic priests had made sacramental wine there. It was standing empty and possibly for sale, and I was thinking about raising money for the Melchizedek priesthood to have a school or center there.

Tom said, "Why would you want to put all that energy into raising money to buy, repair, and heat it? Why not use the energy for a school without walls?"

So that was the end of the idea of a building in a specific location. It makes my work a whole lot easier, and it keeps us mindful of what's important and what isn't.

What Would You Tell Mozart?

One evening, I was doing ordinations in Michigan and one of the people to be ordained was a child of about six years old. His name was Christopher, and he was a Reiki II practitioner. He was barely able to climb up into the ordination seat, but he basically understood what he was about to participate in. As he took his seat, I was aware that there were adults in the room that were questioning to themselves what I was doing ordaining a small child. I am not permitted to refuse anybody, so I knew that having the child there was appropriate.

When I returned home, I called Tom to ask his opinion about what had occurred with this little boy.

Tom said: "Would you tell Mozart not to play the piano at five? There won't be many children, but there will be a few, and those that do, have a knowing of the rightness for them."

On another occasion, in Canada, a little boy was being put into position to be ordained, and one of his parents had filled out the registration form. When the boy crawled up in the seat, he turned to me and said, "Mr. Chesbro, I really don't want to do this." So I said to him, "It's okay. I'll be back another time." The parents were not happy with this, but in this situation, the child had more wisdom than they did.

Over the years there have not been many children come forward for ordinations. Of all who have been ordained, less than 12 have been children.

The World's Greatest Healer

There was an occasion when I had to telepathically call on Tom to help me with a situation in an ordination. This was the only time that I ever had to call on Tom about an ordination, and I was grateful for his help.

A young man arrived dressed in full buckskin regalia, and he called me aside to let me know that he was the world's greatest healer and that he would be levitating while I was doing his ordination. He was accompanied by a very young woman, and they were obviously a couple.

She was called first and was ordained. I could tell spiritually that she shifted from who she was before her ordination, and that she had taken all her power back as a result. The male host of the event gave her a hug to congratulate her, and the man in buckskin bristled upon seeing that. He was to be called next, and I asked Tom what I should do with this situation.

Tom telepathically told me to ask the young man to take the seat and that if he refused, I wouldn't have to ordain him. I called his name and asked him to take the seat, but instead of doing so, he began to shout and yell and curse me. He was not ordained, while the young woman took her power back by taking the ordination.

No Hierarchy

Sometimes people ask questions about the nature of God and angels and so forth. The bottom line is that there is no delineation of the Light. Your soul may have a certain amount of dreams, but all souls are equal to the energy that is God. In the Order of Melchizedek, unlike the evolution in the Christian Church, there is no hierarchy: we have no high priests or priestesses. I believe this is a disappointment for some who want a hierarchy. There are many within the priesthood who follow the teachings and go on to teach. In the time of the Buddha, in the Sangha or school, all were welcome. The original intent of the Melchizedek priesthood was and is to be like a sangha, a Buddhist community of monks, nuns, novices, and laity. We are all one family, with no one greater or lesser than any other. All are equal in the sight of God, and as above so below.

The All-Night Dream

I've been on the road doing ordinations since 1986, and in all the years I have traveled I have never arrived a day ahead of time. On one trip I arrived at my destination, parked the car, and ran in thinking that I was a little late.

My host was surprised and asked, "Dan, what are you doing here?"

And I said, "Gee, I'm sorry, I'm a little bit late."

And she said, "You're a day early!"

She told me about a nice hotel in town and offered me some money to stay there and have a nice meal.

I found the hotel and had a lovely steak dinner and went to bed early. All night I dreamed that I was talking with Tom Sawyer. He said he was somewhat disappointed that the priesthood and the ordinations had not moved forward as far as he had anticipated. I said that I didn't agree with him, and that being in the field doing the ordinations every weekend, I saw a domino effect with each of the people ordained, and how that influence was passed on to thousands of other people.

This dream lasted all night, and we talked all night long. Tom and I apparently needed to have this long conversation in dreamtime. When I got up in the morning, I had the feeling that I had been able to lessen his concern that the work had not gone fast enough or far enough. Later, I realized that my early arrival had not been an accident. At a much later date, he told me that if we had both died, then the work had been done. As I recall the steak was very good.

Order of Melchizedek

One day, Tom called me at home and asked me what I was doing. I told him I was vacuuming, and I asked why he was asking.

He said, "Have you ever gone around the world to see what the priests are doing?"

I said, "No."

He said, "I have. They are doing wonderful work, and if you and I both die right now, we have done our work."

I have learned that before I graduate I will have a dream or a vision concerning whether I pass the responsibility for ordinations on to another or take it Home with me. As of now, I haven't had that dream or vision; that's in the future. I know that I have a long life ahead of me. It is the Canadian priests who seem to be most concerned about what will happen to the Church when I pass. I know this well: the Church will go on.

Neutrinos

Assisting the Research

Several years ago, a small group of us took a trip to Sudbury, Ontario. Tom told me that he was going to be interviewed by a psychologist, and that that person would decide whether to take him to the old nickel mine where they were working on capturing neutrinos (at that point in time these energy forms were not yet identified as neutrinos).

The group of us went into this little room, and some of the group were Melchizedek priests from the Sudbury area. The psychologist came in and was playing "cat and mouse" with Tom to see if he had the facility for understanding physics.

Tom met the necessary expectations, so he was taken to meet the physicists in the old nickel mine, very deep underground. He was aware that they were working with complex mathematical formulas and looking for answers to certain mathematical inquiries.

Tom asked, "Hey, boys, what are you doing with your math?" He had the answers to their math questions, but because of free will he was not permitted to give them answers unless they asked questions.

They probably had to overcome their ego to ask questions of someone with a high school education about the physics they had spent years studying. Tom made an arrangement that when they got stuck they could communicate with him and he would give them the information needed.

Several years later, neutrinos were discovered. Scientists in different locations around the world were all working together to study them.

Tom told me: "What they discovered is that neutrinos have no death cycle; that the Universe is constantly reincarnating. What they will never discover in a test tube is that the nature of neutrinos is Unconditional Love. It is God. At this time the scientists are saying that neutrinos are only 5 percent of the Universe. But they make up 100 percent of the Universe."

Neutrinos do not evolve to become wavelength functions or subatomic particles, but because they exist, they facilitate other building blocks of the Universe to come into existence. It would be as if neutrinos are the foundation of a house. The foundation doesn't evolve to become a house, but the rest of the structure is built on it.

The Neutrino Lunch

After the discovery of neutrinos, Tom and I went to lunch one day and discussed their discovery.

I said, "This is great. There is no difference between you, a rock, and a hard place."

He replied, "Yes!"

Then I asked, "Can't we now have world peace, because it proves that there is no racism, sexism, or classism? We are all One!"

Tom told me that we would create a peaceable kingdom here on Earth with this new awareness, but that Earth is a schoolroom where souls come to learn about Love and Creativity against a background of greed and ego. Then he asked, "Do you want to close the school?"

"No," I replied, "of course not."

He continued: "The Earth is a place of duality, where there will always be greed and ego. As long as souls are coming here, this is what they will bounce up against. We must learn to have compassion for all sentient beings, especially now that we know that we are all One."

Tom joked about a future time when two New Agers will be meeting over coffee, and one will say to the other, "Well, you know, I have more Oneness than you!"

Tom said that the discovery of neutrinos is proof of the unified field in physics. Our bodies are completely saturated with that energy: Unconditional Love.

First Annual Neutrinos Conference

Several years after the discovery of neutrinos, that knowledge is becoming commonplace around the world. The Sudbury priesthood group invited me to come up to their conference and do ordinations. When we pulled into the entranceway to Laurentian University in Sudbury, Ontario, there was a large banner at the entrance that said, "Welcome to the First Annual Neutrinos Conference," and I thought how much fun that would be to go over and talk to those people and tell them how that was facilitated with Tom's input.

We went over, but without a registrant's badge we weren't allowed in. Perhaps one of those who attended that conference will read this book and appreciate how the process of that discovery unfolded.

Travels

The Blue Light of Christ

One of the things Tom and I worked on together was going to sacred places around the planet in proximity to 33 degrees north latitude to anchor the Blue Light of Christ. This task was to help with the healing of the planet and had to be completed by the end of 1992. The 33 degrees north latitude is vulnerable to volcanoes and earthquakes.

The mission to anchor the Blue Light started at the Great Pyramid in Egypt and ended there as well (a few of the places are quite a distance from the 33 degrees parallel). These places included Stonehenge in England; the Universal Hall Building in the Findhorn Community in Scotland; Sedona, Arizona; Los Angeles, California (on a hill above the Paramahansa Yogananda Meditation Garden); Hawaii; and Lhasa, Tibet– to name but a few. Tom believed that in order to finish this work he had to be ordained into the Order of Melchizedek, which took place on September 15, 1991. He told me it would have been sacrilegious to participate in the encircling of the Blue Light and the Great Pyramid final ceremony had this not been done.

A small group of priests, including Tom, anchored the Blue Light in Lhasa, Tibet. We were meeting the larger group of priests in Cairo on November 21, 1991, to complete the circumnavigation of the Blue Light in a final ceremony in the Great Pyramid on November 22. This was the completion of four years of anchoring the Blue Light.

Tom and I were talking one night and discussing the mission of the Blue Light. He asked me, "Well, you're not trying to ruin the plan, are you?" He was referring to the millions of people who had near-death experiences around the world who were assisting, and all the other things being done, and asking if I was planning to change that or confirm the plan for circumnavigating the globe. His question takes on greater significance in the story that follows.

Events at the Potala Palace and Chokpuri Hill

Two or three years before we were able to go to Tibet, I had a dream of being in a room with candles burning everywhere and a golden mandala in the middle of the floor. There were two Buddhist monks in the room and two other people dressed in indigo blue. Four tall, square columns supported the room. The message from the dream was that we were to go to Lhasa to anchor the Blue Light at that location.

Prior to going to Tibet, one of the priests had an opportunity to visit with the Dalai Lama, who was in California at the time. She asked him about the trip to Lhasa. The Dalai Lama said it was not necessary to go there physically, and that it could be dangerous due to the Chinese occupation.

A couple of years later, despite the warning from the Dalai Lama, I felt it necessary that we have a physical presence there to do the ceremony. We left Katmandu on the way to Lhasa on this large jet. Once in the air, I suddenly felt all the energy drain out of my body. I couldn't move and could barely speak. My friend John was seated across the aisle. He looked over and recognized that I was in great distress and helped me up and walked me to the restroom.

From that point on, the memories I have do not coincide with reality much. My memory is that I used the facility and then lay on the floor in the restroom. There were six other people standing over me, two of them all in white. They were having a conversation and asking, "Is he going to be alright?" Then John moved me to a window seat, where I was able to look out at the Himalayas.

My perception of the trip was that it took about half an hour, but Tom later told me that it was three and a half hours, so three hours are missing from my memory altogether. When the plane landed, my feet had already turned black. Tom was pinching the back of my neck to keep my life force going, a method jujitsu masters use to keep you in your body, as he and John helped me off the plane. My next memory is of looking down a long tunnel as my friend was helping me into the Holiday Inn at Lhasa.

Later that night, Tom came to my room to check on me. I asked him, if I was incapable would he be able to go to the garden in front of the Potala Palace and anchor the Light. He replied, "Son, whatever you ask me to do, I will do."

His reply answered two questions for me: (1) that he would do the ceremony tomorrow in Lhasa if I couldn't, and (2) that he was spiritually permitted to participate in the ceremony in the Great Pyramid in a few days. I had been concerned about Tom's participation in the ceremony and whether it would interfere with his destiny, as he had told me that he had to meet with a man outside the Great Pyramid.

As a youth I was sick a lot. I had a teddy bear that I kept with me. The doctors would turn both me and the bear over to give us shots of penicillin. I spent a lot of time hugging that bear, as it calmed my anxiety and fears. Tom brought me a small pillow that he had along with him to help with his back problem and threw it on the credenza in my room. When he left, I crawled out of bed, got the pillow, brought it to bed, and fell asleep hugging it. It was like having my teddy bear for comfort again. The next morning I felt totally fine, and went looking for Tom to return his pillow. He was sitting in the hotel restaurant, having breakfast, and as I handed him the pillow, he said, "Oh, you drained it!"

After breakfast, a group of priests and I took a trip to a mountain-top monastery. Tom stayed behind with Warren, a priest who wasn't feeling well. As we looked back down the mountain toward Lhasa, we saw that it was shrouded in mist. We realized later that we were looking at air pollution from the many motorized rickshaws that ran through the city. Prior to 1959, there was no air pollution in Lhasa.

In the monastery courtyard, we gathered in a circle for a celebration ceremony and to sing. As we gathered, a bee appeared and flew around us. I thought it odd that it would be at such a high altitude, especially in November.

We went down the mountain, met the others, and proceeded to the garden park to anchor the Blue Light. When we returned to the hotel, Tom asked me if I had noticed all the monks and nuns who had gathered to watch us. I replied, "No, I didn't notice." Several months later I received photographs someone took of the celebration ceremony, and they contained the many monks and nuns who had gathered.

Years later, I learned from Tom that he would often use a bee or a dog to keep an eye on me. He said, "I want to make sure you're okay." Obviously, it was Tom looking through the eyes of the bee to notice the monks and nuns, while at the same time he was with Warren in the Holiday Inn.

Later that day, we anchored the Blue Light in two locations: first in a ceremony in a garden in a park in front of the Potala Palace and then in a small room at the shrine of the Buddha that was dedicated to women. This was the first location of a temple to Buddha in Tibet and was the holiest place in Lhasa. The shrine is in a cave in Chokpuri Hill, which had been used as the basement of a Tibetan monastery hospital. The hospital on top of Chokpuri Hill was built by the first Tibetan doctor to come to Lhasa. That hospital was destroyed in the Chinese invasion and was later replaced with radio antennas.

Sanjar, our tour guide, had arranged for us to go and look for the holy place to do the second ceremony. The first place we went was down a dirt road, and when we went around a corner we had our first encounter with Chinese soldiers. They were relieving themselves in the bushes.

We then went up the stairs on the side of Chokpuri Hill to a monastery. There, in a room, were candles burning everywhere, square pillars, and two monks; however, I wasn't convinced it was the right place, because in my dream the event took place at night and there was a golden mandala on the floor. We went into a little chapel adjacent to the first room, a chapel dedicated to women, and there were Buddhist women praying there. But we left the chapel and went back down the stairs on the side of the hill.

Tom had gone down the stairs ahead of us and was standing in front of a thick red door. He was looking at the door as if he could see through it. He saw an L-shaped room behind the door, but he couldn't see around the corner of the "L." The door had obviously been locked for a long time, and no one had a key.

So we left Chokpuri Hill and went to the national hospital, because it had a basement and we knew that there were pictures of mandalas on the walls. But they wouldn't let us in.

Tom asked, "Dan, what do you want to do?"

I said, "It feels like we should go back to the first place."

So we went back to Chokpuri Hill and the monastery. When we got there, all the Chinese soldiers were gone (we never saw them again). Once more, we proceeded up the stairs to the monastery.

When we walked into the room, there were the two monks there, with candles burning, and they pointed to the spot where there were semi-precious stones embedded in the floor in the form of a cross. They indicated to us, by pointing to the symbol, that we could prostrate ourselves in prayer upon the stones. The stones lined up with the higher chakras. This was a very sacred spot, and we each took turns prostrating ourselves. Then we did a Melchizedek meditation and anchored the Blue Light.

As we were leaving, the monks gave us little balls of dough that they give to pilgrims. When we got to the bottom of the stairs Tom noticed that the thick red door to the L-shaped room was open. In the L-shaped room to the left was an altar with remnants of a golden Buddha on it. I went into an adjacent room accompanied by two young monks. There was a single light bulb illuminating the room, and there were puddles on the floor that the young monks and I playfully skipped in.

Then I heard crying and went back into the room where Tom was. He was asking our Chinese female guide, Willy, "When was the earthquake?" She said, "It happened the year I came to school here."

Tom said, "Yes, and it changed the water table" (which accounted for the puddles). Tom was weeping and had his hand on a crack in the wall in the L-shaped room.

He said, "When I died, God told me that the New Age would begin by a series of earthquakes and volcanoes, and one of the earthquakes would crack the Holy Mountain. Why am I like Doubting Thomas, questioning what God had told me and putting my hand in the wound?"

When Tom had initially looked through the door with his "x-ray vision," he could see that the cave was filled with refuse. He could see that it was an L-shaped room, but he could not see around the corner as junk was being stored in the hallway entrance. It was sad to see that in one of the holiest places in all of Tibet. Tom later said that maybe we should offer to go and clean it out, but that never happened.

So my dream was fulfilled. We found the holy place, two monks, the burning candles, the square columns, and the golden mandala being the semi-precious stones on the floor. That part of the assignment was complete.

Hugging Caveat

We were traveling through India with Tom on one of our spiritual journeys, and we were a happy and hugging bunch. While traveling through a big city, Tom cautioned us about hugging strangers.

He said: "Hugging may not be culturally appropriate, and besides, you don't have the immunities to certain germs from their environment. You could contract a sickness that you have no immunity for or give them a sickness they can't fight. Give them food or money as a gesture of friendship, but be cautious about hugging strangers in another country."

Be Compassionate and Allow Them to Die Pain-Free

When the priesthood took a trip to India and Tibet, Tom went with us. We encountered many beggars, many very poor and starving people. In one situation we were on a tour bus, and a starving woman and her baby approached the side of the bus. She was utterly emaciated and holding her hand out for food.

Tom directed us, saying: "Don't feed them. The baby will die in a day or two from starvation, and she will, too. But if you feed her now, she will die in excruciating agony because she hasn't eaten in so long. I know how all of you on this bus cannot understand how this could be an act of compassion not to feed her or her baby. Please understand that this is the truth."

Now, I ask you, who but a Christed being would have the level of awareness to know that this person would die within a day or two, and the compassion to allow her to die pain-free?

On the Jokhang Temple

On our last day in Lhasa, Tom arranged for us to do an ordination on the roof of the Jokhang Temple.

The woman being ordained was called Jo (Tom said that Buddha's nickname was "Joh"). It was a bright, sunny November day, and we found a sawhorse on the roof of the temple, and that was suitable as a place for Jo to sit. Tom held the cup and the other implements for ordination as I completed the ceremony.

There is a Jewish prophecy that when the Messiah comes He will stand on the roof of the temple. There is no temple standing in Jerusalem today, but then the prophecy didn't state which temple He would stand on.

The following day we left Tibet to join our friends in Egypt.

Tools in the Pyramid

Before we took the priesthood to Egypt, in 1991, I had dreams about what I was to do in the Great Pyramid. Tom came over one evening, and I explained to him what the dreams had asked me to do.

He said, "You know, there are tools in there for you to use. Take the pyramid and turn it, and look at it from different angles, and what do you see?"

I had been inside the pyramid once or twice before and had seen a ladder leaning up against the wall on the way to the Queen's Chamber. I was thinking that maybe that was a tool.

He said, "No, look at it again."

I kept looking at it from many different angles, then I realized that the tool was the sarcophagus in the King's Chamber. The initiates went into the sarcophagus to overcome all their fears. When they had mastered their fears, they could go forth and teach.

Ceremony in the Great Pyramid

We arrived in Cairo and met a larger contingent of our priesthood friends. There were over 120 people participating. In the ballroom of the hotel, we held a rehearsal in preparation for the ceremony. The following evening, we all dressed in white, put an element of gold on our heads, and boarded buses to the Great Pyramid. We walked single file into the pyramid to anchor the Blue Light. This would complete the circumnavigation of the planet.

We gathered in the King's Chamber, and everyone took their rehearsed position. Tom's role in this was to be the keeper of the Violet Flame, and he held a purple candle to symbolize this. The ceremony was completed after midnight on November 22, 1991.

Tom had asked the Seneca Nation back home to pray during two holy days: one during the ceremony in the pyramid, and the other when the initiations were being done in the pyramid. As a result, it was both awesome and as easy as could be.

When Tom left the Great Pyramid, he had his prearranged meeting with a man outside, and the following day he flew back to New York. Before departing, he told me that he was restless to leave Egypt, for it was not as he remembered it—lush and green and full of roses and fruit trees; that now it is all sand and dust.

After Tom left, our group continued our planned tour. One of the tour stops was Heliopolis, which was an ancient center of healing. In its day, the temple in the City of the Sun had been one of the Holy of Holies on this planet. However, over the years, it had become the local city dump. We went there expecting it to be great, but now this ancient holy site is used for garbage. As an aside, Edgar Cayce talked about Joseph (of the coat of many colors) marrying the daughter of the High Priest of Heliopolis.

It is ironic and tragic that, over time, two of the holiest places on the planet—the cave in Chokpuri Hill and the temple at Heliopolis—have become garbage dumps. This situation is a metaphoric statement about humanity: one day we are in a holy place, and the next we are in a dump, and that it is due to the choices we make. We are the cause of all our effects.

Two Pregnancies

When we were traveling in Egypt in 1991 with the 133 people, we went to the Temple at Karnak, where there was a stone statue of Sekhmet, with the body of a virgin and the head of a lion. In Egyptian mythology, if you want a child, touching Sekhmet will enhance your ability to get pregnant. You can also ask her questions: if the answer is yes, a smile appears on her face, and if it is no, then a tear appears in her eye.

There were two women traveling with us who wanted to get pregnant. They both went up and touched Sekhmet.

Tom said something to them about getting pregnant: "If I were you and was not totally positive I wanted to have a baby, I wouldn't be messing with touching statues!"

Nine months later, they both had baby girls. Tom was instrumental in helping one of them decide against having an abortion.

The Return Trip

We were on our way home through London, and my former wife, Carol, was trying to coordinate tickets at the ticket counter. Some of our children were with us, and all of us were tired and anxious to return home, when around the corner came a tall, stately Indian gentleman, who spoke to the ticket person and Carol and then left.

She came and told me that we had just been upgraded to first class. We were called to come and take our seats first, in lovely leather seats, and we were given wine and lobster and all kinds of wonderful treats.

When we got home, Tom picked us up. He had a station wagon to accommodate us and all the luggage. While Tom drove, I was remembering that the lobster on the plane was rather tough, but I thought, "Who's going to complain?"

Minutes from arriving back at my farm, Tom said to me, "That lobster was really tough, wasn't it?" I figured Carol had spoken to him about the food.

The next morning I asked her if she had told him about the food on the plane, and she said, "No, I didn't tell him a thing."

Later I spoke with Tom about the tall Indian man who had upgraded us to first class, and Tom's only reply was, "Well, you had worked so hard and you deserved it."

Extraordinary Abilities

Boyhood Abilities

Tom demonstrated extraordinary abilities even before his first death experience at 33 years of age. In the early part of his life he didn't believe in God, even though he already possessed unusual abilities, such as reading auras, receiving telepathic thought, and knowing of a plane crash that was about to occur so that he could ride his bike to the airport in order to give spiritual assistance to those who asked for it. For Tom, these were normal experiences. He didn't realize then what he possessed, or what part he played as a messenger. For example, when Tom was playing in the sandbox with his friends as a boy, he was able to read the thought forms in their auras. Even though he didn't believe in God, he had exceptional experiences with heightened abilities.

Remember Sitting on the Rafters?

Many years after Tom had been on my TV show and we had become friends, he and our friend Al were at my home helping me fix the pump in my well. The pump had to be pulled out of the ground, and it took all three of us to do it. Back when I bought the farmhouse it needed to be gutted, and I would sit up on the rafters on the second floor and look down through the skeletal structure at the bottom floors and imagine where doors and windows should be placed. I was physically alone when I did that. When Tom was leaving the afternoon after we finished my well, he asked me, "Do you remember when we used to sit up on the rafters and look down through the floors?" I agreed that it had been fun, but after he left I realized that I hadn't even met him at that time but he was already aware of me, spiritually hanging out with me while I was sitting on the rafters.

The Couple Stuck in the Snow

There was a beauty parlor, Pal Joey's, in Rochester, New York, where Tom would teach after hours. He would bring a briefcase full of papers and fumble through them as the group assembled. There were always questions, all kinds of questions. One night while Tom was teaching, he periodically looked at his watch, and somebody finally asked him why. He said that a couple was going to get stuck in the snow under a bridge, but it hadn't happened yet. It was snowing heavily, so he encouraged us to go home early, saying that it was time for him to go and help these kids get out of the snow. It was amazing that he was aware that they were going to be stuck before they did.

The Best-Tasting Apple

One time, around Rosh Hashanah, a few of us came together to celebrate the Jewish holiday. It's traditional to dip apples in honey and eat them, as apples aid good health and the honey symbolizes the hope for a sweet year. We passed around apple slices, and everyone was to share one of the sweetest experiences that had happened to them in the past year. It was the best-tasting apple I had ever had. The next day, I was doing a workshop at Unity Church in Rochester and Tom unexpectedly walked in. He looked at me and said with a smile that that was the best-tasting apple he had ever had last night—but he hadn't been there! He had the ability to sense what others sensed. It was rather extraordinary that he could do that.

The Sleeping Pilot

One of Tom's abilities was to know about situations involving aircraft. Part of his mission was to take care of such things, mostly in North America, but it could be around the world as well. In one instance, a pilot had fallen asleep in flight and was on a collision course with another aircraft. Tom, being aware that was happening, and knowing of the probability of a collision, whispered in the pilot's ear: "You are a really good pilot. You should be proud of your ability and how good you are." By doing this and encouraging the pilot to feel good about himself, the pilot awoke from his slumber, sat up, saw the approaching plane, and avoided a mid-air collision.

Plane Crash

From his death experience and having Total Knowledge of all probable futures, Tom was aware of the potential crash of an L-1011 plane in Texas. He went through the scenario over and over in his head, and felt a lot of angst about wanting to prevent the crash. Through Spirit, he knew a lot of details about it—the plane, the weather on the day of the crash, and the names of all the passengers and crew.

While talking on the phone with a professor at the University of Connecticut, Tom exclaimed, "Oh, my God, it's happening!" and got off the phone. On final approach, the plane was caught in a wind shear. Tom was spiritually in the plane as the crew lost control of the aircraft and present with the people as they experienced those fear-filled moments before and during the crash.

The plane bounced off the runway, hitting a car being driven on a side road. The man driving the car was going to work, elated over his birthday party the night before. He had taken an alternative route to work that day, different from the one he always drove. The last thing he saw was a big black tire coming through the windshield. The plane bounced back up, landed in a field, and burst into flames. Tom guided some of the passengers out of the wreckage. It was incredible that he had the ability to go out of his body to assist the survivors.

Ghosts on L-1011s

Sometimes usable parts from retired or crashed planes are recycled for use in aircraft currently in service. According to the story that Tom shared, the spirit of the pilot and flight engineer of a crashed L-1011 attached themselves to the recycled materials in other planes. Their ghosts appeared to many flight crew members and passengers (for the complete story, read Ghosts of Flight 401 by John G. Fuller). Several people had conversations with them, and they sometimes gave warnings about specific parts. These sightings continued until the airlines removed every single recycled part of the crashed plane from all the aircraft that had them. Tom talked about "his" planes as if they belonged to him. He had tremendous admiration for the engineering involved in building an aircraft and was passionate about not wanting another L-1011 crash to occur.

Uncle Joe

Tom and I were in Virginia at a conference, and he was asked to be a presenter. I told the people going to listen to him to bring tape recorders, sleeping bags, and to do him a favor by making sure he ate and went to the bathroom. He talked for three days and nights. One night, some of us were going out for coffee, and I was running down the hall on my way. He greeted me in the hall as I passed, saying, "See you later, Uncle Joe." It almost stopped me in my tracks, as I had had a spiritual insight into something that had happened in the life of Jesus.

Joseph of Arimathea was Jesus's uncle, and it was Joseph's tomb where Jesus was laid after his crucifixion and from whence he was resurrected. Joseph was a tin merchant, and he was very wealthy. He had mines in what would become southern Spain and was well connected to the Romans and the Roman Empire. The members of the Sanhedrin in Jerusalem respected him, and it is probable that he was a member himself.

As a very young man, Jesus had gone to India with him and worked with the Jains. Jesus then went north, where he met the Hindus. To put it mildly, Jesus was not in favor of the caste system and so they wanted to destroy him. He quickly left on horseback with his uncle and rode north to a place called Hemis in northern India/Tibet. He came to be called St. Issa by the Buddhists and was revered for his spiritual wisdom.

Later he and his Uncle Joseph went to Turkey to meet the Zoroastrians (in a previous incarnation he had been Zend, father of Zoroaster). Following that, they went on to Greece and then England, where they met the Druids.

At one point in my life, I had a dream in which I was instructed to trace the steps of Joseph of Arimathea. I went to Hemis, Stonehenge, the Great Pyramid, and Malaga, where the tin mines were located. "Uncle Joe" was someone I was aware of from my dreams, but I had never talked to Tom about why I had gone to those places. I found it amazing that he knew everything, even my most private thoughts and dreams. "See you later, Uncle Joe."

The Prophecy Fulfilled

One morning I received a phone call from Tom. During our short conversation, he said, "As of May 23, 1978, the Jewish prophecy has been fulfilled, and they are no longer the chosen people."

His death experience had happened on that date, and that is what he was referring to. Elijah, or the Messiah the Jewish people were expecting, had not come; instead, what had come was that energy—in the form of Tom Sawyer.

Tom's middle name, Joseph, means "and God will add." When Tom died on that day he was overshadowed by God's Spirit, and what came back to the Earth plane was a messenger to serve as a bridge between the Age of Pisces and the Age of Aquarius. Tom's return from the dead was the fulfilling of that prophecy and the coming of the Messiah.

Teaching the Teacher

Tom and I were in his kitchen talking one evening, when he said, "It's exciting for me to be teaching my teacher." Then he asked, "Don't you remember when we were in Turkey or Glastonbury together?" It was a rhetorical question. It was fun for me to contemplate that I had been his teacher at some point, and now he was mine.

The King David Boundaries

We were at the beauty parlor one evening, and Tom was teaching. It was during the Middle East crisis in the 1980s.

Tom said, "You know that when the boundaries of Israel return to what they were in the time of King David, it will usher in a long period of world peace."

I keep anticipating that that will take place, despite all the tensions and grievances between the peoples in the Middle East. Still, I have no doubt whatsoever that when the boundaries return to what they were, we will have peace.

Greasy Cheeseburgers

Oftentimes, on my way home from doing a workshop, part of my grounding process was to get a big greasy cheeseburger.

One day, Tom was talking to a group of teenagers at my home, and he said, "And there are some people who consider themselves to be spiritual, but they stop on the way home to eat greasy cheeseburgers."

Tom knew, although I had never told anyone. Again, I was amazed at what he was able to know just by tuning in.

Speak Their Language

Often when Tom met with people (especially young people) he would speak their language. Though he rarely used obscenities, if every other word started with "f" or whatever, he would be right in there with them. He had the ability to become invisible yet one with them by using their vernacular.

Another example of his ability to connect was when he saw a young person playing a guitar. That person was playing a very unusual chord, and Tom knew the significance of it and commented on it to him. The young person was impressed and later said to me, "Hey, Mr. Chesbro, that Tom Sawyer is a cool dude."

I've never known anyone who had such an ability to communicate by entering the other person's model of the world the way Tom did. What a wonderful ability.

The Power of Prayer

Tom told us about an event that had happened in the Middle East, in which terrorists had commandeered a plane and forced it to land. The terrorists attempted to negotiate with the authorities by trying to swap passengers for prisoners who were being held in Israeli prisons. Of course, the Israelis would not negotiate with terrorists.

On the plane, the terrorists were going seat by seat looking for Jews. During that process, they were molesting and beating some of the passengers. One of the passengers was a young woman from Minnesota who was in the Middle East teaching in a school for disabled children. She watched as one by one the terrorists called certain passengers up to the front of the plane, shot them in the head, and pushed their body onto the tarmac. They intended to kill passengers until their demands were met. A German woman was shot in the head and pushed off the plane, and as she lay dying on the tarmac her body was twitching. A couple of the terrorists ran down the steps from the plane and shot her until she stopped moving. The young Minnesota woman decided that if she was shot, she would pretend to be dead and lie perfectly still.

That day, Tom Sawyer was working at his job, raking asphalt, when he became spiritually aware of these events. He went out of body and traveled to the site and went seat by seat to see if anyone was praying or asking God for help. The young woman from Minnesota was the only person on the plane who was praying and asking God for help, so she was the only one that Tom could help. Once again, this is a situation that shows that God will not interfere in your sacred space and free will, but because the young woman had prayed to God, Tom went to be with her.

He whispered words of comfort to her, telling her that everything was going to be okay. She was taken to the front of the plane and shot in the head, but the bullet acted like a cork and lodged in her skull. Like the others, she was thrown off the plane, and although not dead she pretended to be dead. While she was lying beneath the plane, pretending to be dead, her grandmother, who was in spirit, came to her. She told her that she could survive the incident, but in doing so, she would end up divorced and semi-paralyzed and would have to go through therapy. Alternatively, she could choose to go with her grandmother and pass over. She had to make a choice. When she made the decision that she would stay, Tom left (spiritually).

As the event unfolded, soldiers rushed the plane and shot some of the terrorists when they rescued the remaining people. The young woman ended up being put in the same truck as the man who had shot her. She made a moaning sound, and they realized that she wasn't dead. Then she was taken to a hospital and placed in the same room as the man who had shot her.

Much later, this young woman was on a panel of near-death experiencers on the Phil Donahue Show, where she related her story. She told the audience that she did not hate the man who shot her, and the audience booed her for saying that. Tom Sawyer was also on the same panel that day, and he was worried that she would recognize him. His concern was that she had prayed to God for help, and had gotten Tom instead. But at one point during the show she commented to Phil Donahue about Tom, saying, "Isn't he a wonderful guy!" She didn't recognize him as the person who spoke to her telepathically on the plane.

This woman had to undergo extensive physical therapy for her physical challenges and she and her husband did indeed divorce; however, she remarried, and with her new husband went on to travel extensively and teach survival. A couple of years after the Phil Donahue Show, she was scheduled to teach where Tom Sawyer lived. Tom was again anxious that she might find him. He was always afraid that she might think that God had not helped her, but in truth, Tom was God's messenger in this event, as he was in so many others.

Sitting on the Ganges

On the first part of our trip to Tibet and Egypt, we went to India. We went to Nepal and to the headwaters of the Ganges, Rishikesh, one of my favorite places. We were staying at a really nice hotel, and along with the Hindu priests, we were making little boats out of leaves and sending them down the Ganges.

A couple in our group had gotten into a little relationship difficulty and wanted me to counsel them, so we were up on a balcony talking about their issues. Meanwhile, Tom had put on a black t-shirt and bathing suit and swam out to the middle of the Ganges. There, people witnessed him standing up and walking around on top of the river and then sitting on the water in a lotus position, meditating and praying—he said that it would have looked like someone sitting in the middle of the river.

Years later, I came across a couple of pictures of Tom sitting on the Ganges. One meaning of "sawyer" is a twig in the river, and because it's there, it changes the course of the river forever. So Tom Sawyer sat on the River Ganges, and when the holy water encountered him, it changed course. All this was a metaphor for him being a twig in the stream of consciousness, changing history forever.

The water at Rishikesh is fresh from the Himalayan Mountains and is the result of melting ice and snow. Most humans could never withstand the water temperature (about 38 degrees), yet Tom swam in it, and there he sat on top of it, doing his prayers in a lotus position.

Symbolically, this act was about his life, coming into the Earth plane, leaving his mark, and as a result changing the stream of consciousness and the history of the human condition (he prevented nuclear war and did a lot of work overseeing the Gulf War, just to name two). When the United States government investigated him, they said he was the most unusual person they had ever investigated. It sure was fun to travel with him.

In the Heat or in the Cold

Tom's body was unusual in that it didn't sweat. In the Great Pyramid, there were many people in the King's Chamber who were dripping wet from the heat; the energy generated was so great that even the walls were sweating and the purple candle Tom was holding melted in his hand. But still he did not sweat. Then again, Tom could stand out in freezing weather in only short sleeves or swim in 38-degree water and not be cold.

Tom the Actor

Occasionally, I would go over to Tom's place, and we would discuss things over coffee, but he and I did not spend considerable time together until we went to Egypt and India. He would say, "You know, I am really an actor." He told me that he could have called on 12,000 people to assist him in his work, but he had chosen not to do it that way. I had a concern that someone might harm him for their own glorification, but he said not to worry because that situation would never happen.

Mr. Sawyer versus Classical Music

When Tom Sawyer returned from the hospital after his first death experience, he lay on his couch for three days and three nights. During this time he listened to the radio. His wife liked to listen to classical music, and before his death experience Tom did not. In fact, he used to come into the room and turn off the radio or change the station if classical music was playing.

One day during his recovery he asked his wife to turn the radio on, and when she realized that it was tuned to classical music she rushed back to turn it off or change the channel. The composition being played was by Joseph Haydn, and Tom said to her, "That's Joe talking to God, and God responding." By having access to Total Knowledge he knew everyone intimately, so Haydn was "Joe" to him.

At another point, a composition by Antonio Vivaldi was being broadcast, and from his death experience, as with Haydn, Tom had come to know Vivaldi intimately. Vivaldi was a very sickly child. His family groomed him to become a Catholic priest, but because he was so sickly he was not allowed to perform mass; instead, they locked him in a room in an orphanage and commanded him to create music. In a previous life, apparently Tom took the form of a female named Felicity, who was compelled to sing in an orphanage choir. Vivaldi composed the sacred music for the church-run orphanage. When this composition came on, Tom knew the alto part and sang along with the chorus in falsetto. It is possible that Tom did not like classical music prior to his first death experience, because in that past life, as Felicity, he was forced to sing classical music in the choir.

No Keys

Tom called one afternoon and asked me to come over to his place. While we were in the kitchen chatting, he walked across the floor, and picked up the phone and started to talk to someone who had called for help on their marital problems—but the phone had not rung before he picked it up.

Tom asked me, "How would you like to see my son skipping school?"

So we got in his car and drove over to the school parking lot. As we arrived, his son was walking out of the school and got into his truck. He stuck some chewing tobacco into his mouth and then looked up and noticed that his dad and I were sitting across from him in the parking lot.

He bent over and spat out the tobacco and came over to his dad's car and asked, "Dad, what are you doing here?"

Tom replied, "What are you doing skipping school?"

His son said, "I'm going to pick up my tux for the prom."

And Tom said, "No. Go get that after school. I will leave the car, but I need the truck to go and get something for Uncle Al."

His son went back into school, and we got in the truck and drove down the road a couple of miles.

Then Tom said, "Oh, I guess I need keys for the truck." That's when I realized there were no keys in the ignition, but the truck was running fine.

We drove back to Tom's house to get a set of keys for the truck, and when he stopped, the engine turned off by itself. He got the keys, restarted the truck, and we proceeded to go to the hardware store to get stockade fencing for Al.

On the way, Tom said, "When we get there, the young man is going to tell me that the fencing is not all going to fit inside the back of the pickup truck, but it will—and I am not doing magic."

We got to the hardware store, and the young man said, "I don't know how to tell you, but the fencing is not going to fit in the back of your pickup truck."

We got the fencing, loaded it, and it took up every inch, but it did fit.

We then went to meet Al for coffee at the restaurant where he worked as a cook. We were an hour late, and I thought it wasn't going to happen, but Tom said not to worry, that Al would be ready just when we got there.

Al was just coming out of the kitchen as we walked through the door. His boss had arrived unexpectedly for a meeting in the kitchen, and only now was Al free to meet us for coffee. The three of us had coffee and then Tom and I drove back to his house, driving into the sunset, which was beautiful. It made me feel really good, and I thought that the human race was going to make it. I glanced over at Tom, and he looked at me and smiled.

Tens of Thousands of Melchizedek Priests

In the early days of the development of the Order of Melchizedek, we would have a spring and summer event at either a hotel or college. At one of the spring events, someone asked Tom how many people would be in the order? He talked about the tens of thousands in the order already who will never take on a physical body. The priests that are here, on the Earth plane, are those who wanted to take on physical form, and it is our job to be in the physical; however, there are tens of thousands of others who are working with us who are not in physical form. This means that if we need help from any dimension, we only need to ask and that is facilitated.

Chaos Theory

One day, Tom was teaching us about a concept in physics called Chaos Theory.

He said to me, "You know, Chesbro, you would not be able to do the math of this or the fine details, but you do have the ability to take the main points and teach it simply."

Sometime later, physicists were working on Chaos Theory, but Tom had conveyed the ideas to us years earlier.

A Trip to Kentucky

Tom was often asked to go to different parts of the country to speak about his death experience. He was invited to Kentucky, and he told me later that 700 people came to the event, but he had gone because there was one person in particular that he needed to communicate with.

After his talk, he waited to see if that person would come forward. The individual waited until everyone else was gone and then came forward. It is amazing that Tom knew that there was one person with whom he needed to speak, and that he went to Kentucky for that one person and knew to wait for them to come to him.

This story reminds me of the Biblical story of Sodom and Gomorrah, where God was going to destroy the city and the prophet was questioning God's judgment about that (see Genesis 18:20). The prophet asked if he found 50 righteous people in the city, would God still destroy it, and God said He would not. Then the prophet began to lower that number, apparently seeking to save the city with the least number of righteous people there. Finally, he got down to just one person, and God said He would spare the city for that one. But the prophet could not find one righteous person and so the city was destroyed. Tom going to Kentucky for one person is reminiscent of this Biblical story, and I think spectacular.

A Dead Bird

During the early years of the ordinations, a lot of my trips were to North and South Carolina. I used to stay with a friend in Raleigh, North Carolina. Her husband did not believe in metaphysical things and affectionately called us "snake handlers."

Tom was staying at their house on one occasion, and the husband and Tom were having a conversation out on their back patio. Tom was thinking that he would like to do something to show the husband the Love and Power of God when, just at that moment, a bird fell out of the sky dead and into the birdbath.

Now, Tom had the ability to bring the bird back to life, but there was just a moment when that would be possible, and unfortunately, that moment passed, and Tom was not able to demonstrate the power of God in that way. Tom had intended to have the husband experience something extraordinary, but the timing was not right, so he let it pass.

Tom and Animals

Tom often shared stories about how he had a wonderful and unique connection with all animals, and how animals would feel a connection with him. He told a story about a lion that was locked in someone's garage, and he went in and talked to it. There were other stories about testy animals that, when they were around him, were mellow.

Animals are part of God. Even this cat sitting in my lap just now is God in the evolutionary form of a cat expressing Love, as God does. It was amazing how all animals related to Tom and wanted to be close to him. Horses across a field would come galloping to the fence and strain against it just to be as close to him as possible.

One time, Tom was swimming out in the Atlantic Ocean near the Association for Research and Enlightenment at Virginia Beach, when 33 dolphins showed up and swam around him in a circle, talking to him. They told him that they were working hard to maintain world peace but humans were making it very difficult. When Tom swam back to shore, the dolphins followed him as closely as they could, almost beaching themselves to be close to him.

An old man fishing on the shore chastised Tom for swimming out in the ocean. He said, "You know, there are barracuda out there."

On another occasion, Tom was with his eldest son on a military ship out at sea, and suddenly they were being followed by many, many dolphins. One of the sailors exclaimed, "My God, look at all those dolphins!" What they didn't realize was that the dolphins knew that Tom was aboard, and they wanted to be near him.

It's delightful to witness Love responding to Love in an ongoing way when around Tom.

Do You Bleed, Mr. Sawyer?

One night, we were at the beauty parlor where Tom used to give a lot of his talks. He told us about a recent dental appointment he had had.

After the dentist had performed the procedure, he seemed perplexed and asked Tom, "Mr. Sawyer, do you bleed?"

Tom replied, "Why? Do you want me to?"

The dentist explained that while he was doing the procedure, not only did Tom not bleed but he did not breathe, either.

Saving the Dalai Lama

When Tom was a boy, he used to practice throwing a rock at a brick wall over and over in order to hit one particular brick, and he got very good at this skill.

Many years later, the Dalai Lama came to Montreal, Quebec, to bestow the vow of the Bodhisattva to hundreds of people. After teaching the vow of the Bodhisattva, he was invited to give a lecture at St. Joseph's Oratory.

Tom encouraged us all to arrive early at the Oratory and to take our seats in a specific place. As we did so, a man in a tuxedo arrived, carrying a brown paper bag. I thought that maybe it was his lunch and he was a musician because he was so formally attired. He took a seat about four rows behind Tom, my former wife, and me.

The procession started, and as the Dalai Lama and other dignitaries arrived, everyone stood up. At the appropriate time, everyone sat down. As I sat, I received a telepathic message, "If I tell you to stand, stand up." I found out later that my former wife had received the same telepathic message.

I looked past her and over at Tom, and he was holding a camera, "weighing" it in his right hand, as if he was gauging a large stone and getting ready to throw it. So Tom had trained himself from childhood by throwing rocks at a brick wall in readiness for this particular moment.

Later, I found out from Tom that the man in the tuxedo had had a gun in the paper bag. He was planning to remain standing when everyone else sat down and then shoot the Dalai Lama. Tom knew he would have to throw the camera at him if he did not sit down with everyone else. Tom also knew that he had to wait until the very last second to determine if the man would use his free will to restrain himself from shooting.

My former wife and/or I would have taken the bullet had the man been able to shoot, and Tom knew what the probability was. It was as if he knew as a child and that he was training to prevent this assassination. His spiritual life did not begin at 33; he was being trained for certain events in his life well before then. Fortunately, the man sat down.

Tom went down to Kentucky and volunteered to be with the security group for the Dalai Lama because he knew there was going to be another attempt by this man on the Dalai Lama's life. Tom went up to the man and asked if he would help with security, explaining that they were short-handed and could use some help. The man really wanted to be special, so

Tom made him feel special by inviting him to be part of the security team. In this way, the assassination attempt was averted.

I know how much Tom cared for and loved the Dalai Lama. During the Dalai Lama's teaching for the vow of the Bodhisattva, he talked about space particles. Tom said to me that the Dalai Lama was really talking about neutrinos, and that in a few days, he would be meeting with scientists to learn more about them.

Tom told us that neutrinos are unconditional Love, the body of God. Years later, when neutrinos were discovered by various scientists around the globe, they were found to have no death cycle, and we now know that they travel faster than the speed of Light, which is what Love does.

The Tree Remained Green

Tom had a good sense of humor and a fun nature. He also had an amazing facility with almost everything. There was a tree in Tom's yard that stayed green in the fall long past any other tree. It stayed healthy and green, when the leaves on other trees had turned colors and dropped. He told this story as if it could have been his energy, the vibration of him around the property. It was humorous the way he said it, but for whatever reason, that tree stayed green.

Speed Traps

Tom loved automobiles and was constantly fixing cars and customizing them. He also liked to drive fast, but he never got a speeding ticket nor was he arrested. He never actually said it, but he implied that he was sort of invisible and could not be seen on radar. One day he was coming down to visit the farm. On Highway 390, there was a place where loons or egrets used to be, and he pointed out that there were pockets of energy alongside the highway there where you can hardly keep your eyes open.

Moving the Big Rig

Tom's profession was working on road crews. One winter, a piece of heavy equipment slipped off the road and went into an embankment, and he said to his road crew, "Look, boys, why don't you go for coffee and when you return we'll deal with this rig." So the men left for a coffee break.

Although it was winter, Tom took off his coat and shirt and was busy extricating the rig from the ditch when one of the men came back unexpectedly and saw Tom moving it. Normally, it would be physically impossible to do that on one's own, and his co-worker was quite alarmed by what he saw.

Tom never described exactly what he had done, but he did say that it was irresponsible of him to have not taken precautions to ensure that no one would witness such a thing. He promised himself that in the future he would take every precaution to ensure that no one would witness extraordinary events and run the chance that they would be emotionally upset.

Meeting Dr. Ritchie

I had an old Volkswagen, and it would run out of gas because the gas gauge was broken. While waiting for roadside assistance I would listen to the audio tape of Dr. George Ritchie, so I heard his account many times. He was one of the first near-death experiencers to share his story with the public on a large scale.

Dr. Ritchie's experience was during WWII, and he had contracted pneumonia. While they were taking an X-ray of him he died. They put a sheet over him, and he went out of his body, but he wasn't aware that he had died. He left his body, and when he came back to find it, the way he recognized himself was from an insignia ring he wore. (Dr. Ritchie's death experience and his account of it provided a key motivation for Dr. Raymond A. Moody, Jr.'s life work.)

After he left the armed forces, Dr. Ritchie became a psychiatrist and was one of the first persons to work with near-death experiencers. Years later, a friend thought it would be a good idea to invite Dr. Ritchie to Rochester to give a talk and meet Tom Sawyer. When Dr. Ritchie arrived at the hotel and saw Tom across the room, they walked up to each other, embraced, and cried. It was beautiful to witness.

A Slow Start

Tom and I were chatting about his first book, *What Tom Sawyer Learned from Dying*. At that time, everyone was excited that it was out and available, but he already knew what was going to happen with the book and its distribution. He said that sales of the book were going to start very slowly, and people would pass the book around, and that's exactly what happened. Eventually, the book went out of print, but the remaining copies were available until recently.

Tom said that it would reach the people it needed to reach, and that there are ways the book finds the people it needs to find. He told me once that there was one sentence in one chapter on suicide that was written for a specific individual in the hope that they would buy the book, read it, and choose to avoid committing suicide.

Who would know that, except for God?

Helicopter at Niagara Falls

One morning I was in the kitchen and there was a TV news report about a near-accident at Niagara Falls involving a helicopter. Shortly thereafter, I spoke with Tom on the phone. He was fully aware of the incident and involved in helping the situation.

Tom was always aware of anything to do with air traffic. He had this possessiveness and spiritual responsibility for all aircraft. For example, when there was a plane being hijacked in Lebanon he knew about it. He had access to Total Knowledge and often talked about his connection to aircraft and air traffic and problems with certain planes.

It was fascinating to me that he knew every detail of the situation at Niagara Falls and other similar events, even though these details had not been made public.

Everyone I Know

God is Total Knowledge, Compassion, and Unconditional Love. From Tom's death experience with Total Knowledge, he knew everything about everybody, including their fantasies and dreams. Surprising as it may seem, Tom and I didn't see each other much over the years. But then he wouldn't have to, given what he already knew.

I have always had vivid memories of past lives in ancient Israel. I used to think that when I was ready to die, I would go back to Israel, because if I went there I would be killed. However, I had never mentioned those thoughts to anyone, including Tom.

One afternoon at his house, out of the blue, he said, "And then there are those people who believe if they go back to Israel they will be killed."

I was flabbergasted that he knew those thoughts of mine. He had the facility to know everyone on the planet. For example, he knew everyone who went down in the airplane crash in Texas. He said that they were like family to him. He said that Total Knowledge is knowing everyone and equals Compassion. God, who is Total Knowledge, does not judge anyone. A personality is just a small part of the person. It took me a long time to figure it out, but now I know that when Tom died he met everybody who was, is, and who is yet to be born.

One time I asked Tom about his experience of knowing everyone, and he said, "Yes. Pretty awesome, huh?"

The Weather Is A-Changin'

Tom once said that he felt sad for those in our area who had swimming pools because there was going to be so much chilly rain that year. Sure enough, we had a very cool and wet summer. He also said that we will get to the point in the transition to the New Age when places that were desert will bloom and places that bloomed will become desert.

Dark Aura

A friend and I were going to breakfast with Tom, and we had an argument just before meeting him. We put on a smile and greeted Tom that way, but he commented on the dark aura around us because of our argument. If we all had the ability to see auras, it would give us a greater opportunity to acquire and use Compassion when interacting with others.

Supercollider Conductor

When Tom came back from his death experience, as a result of his spiritual augmentation he was given all kinds of formulas and physics information that he did not have before.

One of the clusters of information he possessed was of a supercollider conductor that was to be constructed in Rochester, New York. Eventually, its construction was moved to Texas. Tom was able to provide the necessary information so that it could be fired up and more knowledge be acquired about energy. He did whatever he could to help build understanding of the finer workings of physics.

He did not exhibit his brilliance in high school, however, and received scant formal education afterward, but even without formal training he had greater knowledge than physicists. He was more than willing to tell them anything, but they had to ask—he couldn't just tell them. Once they engaged with him and recognized his authenticity, then information was exchanged, although it may have been challenging for their egos to be getting information from someone so academically inferior.

Shared Senses

Somebody asked Tom once, "Does God need people?"

He replied: "Oh, yes—souls and personalities. God knows Itself from the experiences we are having."

It's as if you had children, and while they are having their experiences you are having them at the same time. This means that whatever sensations you are experiencing, God is also participating in them. Tom would allude to the fact that he had tasted the apple you had eaten the night before, or aromas, or colors; he had the ability to tap into your experiences. There needs to be a receptor or personal common connection that is shared. He could, as God does, experience your life, not only through your intellect but also through your five senses.

Have You Been Probed?

Many years ago, one of my neighbors observed a ball of light about the size of a grapefruit following her car. If she went faster it went faster, and if she went slower it slowed. She arrived home, got out of her car, and started running to her house but fell. Her husband came to the door and also saw the ball of light.

Upon hearing this story, Tom told us that those balls of Light are called "spiritual probes." They are coming to observe you and are similar to a guardian angel or little investigator; they report back to God. Over the years, it's been fun to see how often balls of Light show up in photographs.

It rained on the morning my daughter, Patty, was to get married. Since she wanted to have a garden wedding, I asked Tom (in spirit; he had passed on) if he could help with the weather. Just before the ceremony started, the rain stopped. Following the ceremony and picture taking, it started to rain again. When the photographs were developed there was a big, brilliant ball of Light above the heads of the bride and groom. I believe it was Tom making his presence known.

The Statue of Niels Bohr

One time in Copenhagen, I was walking with my friend Christine, and we came across a statue of Niels Bohr. Tom had often mentioned Niels Bohr, because of his interest in physics.

I said to Christine, "Let's look at the statue of Niels Bohr and mentally send Tom a picture of him."

Later, when I spoke with Tom about what Christine and I had done, he said, "Oh, that's what that was about."

He had picked up the mental image we were sending while he was talking to his daughter-in-law and mistakenly thought that he was supposed to talk to her about Niels Bohr.

The Hawaiian Island

I took Melchizedek priests to Hawaii, where, on May 4, 1989, we anchored the Blue Light. We were at a beach, and looking out over the water we could see a small island that had three palm trees growing out of it. When I got home and went to visit Tom, he pulled out a napkin that had a picture he had drawn of the little island with three palm trees. It was comforting to know that, once again, he was looking out for me.

Tom's Short Psychic Reading Career

Someone asked if Tom would ever consider doing readings or spiritual consultations. I proposed it to him, and he agreed to give it a shot. Everybody wanted to get a reading from him. One by one, they would go in and come out frustrated that all he did was talk about his wife and so on.

He told me later that he could not look in a person's eyes and read for them because he knew too much and was afraid that the information might be detrimental to them. I told the people who had had readings that Tom had basically been speaking in parables, using his own family stories. Still, they were not pleased.

Later, Tom said to me: "I don't know how you do this. I can't do this anymore."

Dead Sea Scrolls

In one of his trance readings, Edgar Cayce had accurately described the terrain where the Dead Sea Scrolls would be found. They were discovered when two kids were throwing rocks into a cave and broke an earthen vessel. They went into the cave and found rolled scrolls from the broken vessel and brought one to a scholar in a nearby town.

The scholar recognized the value of these objects and asked the boys to bring him more, saying he would pay them for it. The clever young boys, eager to maximize their earnings, went back to the cave, tore up the scrolls, and brought them back to the scholar to sell piece by piece.

Once, in New York City, I had the opportunity to do a reading for the daughter of a rabbi who had been working with the Vatican on the scrolls. The rabbi's job was to transfer the Dead Sea Scroll material onto IBM cards. Many of the teachings of Melchizedek formed the basis for the Essene community, and much of that material forms the basis for the Dead Sea Scrolls (some of the scrolls were pertinent to that time only).

The rabbi's daughter told me that when her father had died, all the IBM cards had disappeared. She presented me with a booklet, the cover of which had a photographed copy of a piece of the scrolls. It was the book that her father had worked on.

When I returned from New York City, I brought the booklet to show Tom Sawyer. As a result of his death experience he had the ability to read ancient texts and was able to read the words on the photographed parchment piece. He told me that he would be willing to work on reconstructing the scrolls if that became necessary.

Bees and Canines

Tom said: "You realize that I sometimes use the eyes of a bee or a dog so that I can keep an eye on you and be sure that you are safe." He added, "When you are looking at something, I see what you are looking at and then I connect with you."

When I was teaching in Denmark, a bee flew into the room every day, circled around, and flew out the window.

A girl in the group who was allergic to bee stings said, "Kill the bee."

I said no. When I returned to the States, Tom described everyone who had been sitting in the room at the time.

The last time, I experienced him as a bee was in Salt Lake City, Utah. It was April 27, 2007, the night before his final transition. I was sitting outside by a swimming pool in the early evening when a bee showed up and kept circling my head.

Someone sitting nearby said, "You know, there's a bee flying around your head."

I just laughed and said, "Oh, it's a friend of mine."

I knew Tom was not well at the time, but I didn't know that he was ready to make his transition.

The next morning, I woke up and Spirit instructed me to talk about Tom. While teaching the Ordination class, I let it roll and spoke about him more than I usually did. The following day in class, some people asked if I could talk more about "that guy."

It wasn't until I got home that I got the message that Tom had passed. I feel very blessed that he had come one more time as a bee and demonstrated his care for me. I never grieved for Tom, as I know that he isn't gone. Now he is free of his physical body and can be anywhere and everywhere. He taught and demonstrated that there is no death.

Transition and Graduation

Incident on the Plane to Tibet

Tom and I would occasionally go out for a dinner of liver and onions. On one of those occasions, I asked him about what had happened on our flight to Tibet when I had become ill. I remember lying on the floor in the aircraft's restroom, but realize that it was a spiritual experience I was remembering, an enhancement.

My ex-wife was confused about why I would have died on that trip, because I had not completed my work. Tom told her that there was a night when I was driving home from work, when I was tired and crying from exhaustion. While driving to my residence, I had said out loud, "I'm tired, and I just want to go Home." The Universe had heard my plea and had responded to my desire.

Spirit told Tom in a dream that unless he went on this trip, I was going to go Home, in compliance with my stated wish. Tom went on the trip knowing that he could keep me here; otherwise, I would have died on the plane.

Death Experience No. 2

Tom needed surgery to correct his spine which, over time, had been injured from his work. Surgery was scheduled in the spring of 1991, but he didn't want anyone to know about it or interfere.

I was sitting in bed at home, reading a chapter about Joshua in Glen Sanderfur's book, *Lives of the Master*, when Tom called and asked me, "What are you doing?"

I said, "I'm reading Glen Sanderfur's book—the chapter on Joshua."

He said, "Well that's interesting, because I'm reading the book *Joshua* by Joseph F. Girzone." Then he added: "Except for the very beginning and end of this book, this is my story, but I am not Joshua."

What Tom was saying was that he was not Jesus, but that he had god-like abilities and that it was his job to do certain things that Jesus would have done had He returned.

Tom asked me if I would return the book, *Joshua*, to Sidney Farr, author of *What Tom Sawyer Learned from Dying*. I was taking the book to Sidney in Kentucky when a message came through to me on the plane that I could be spiritually present in the operating room during Tom's back surgery so Tom wouldn't die.

While I was with Sidney she called Tom, and he asked to speak to me. He said, "What you were told on the plane—yes to all of that—but don't tell anyone, because we can't have any interference."

On the morning of the operation it was cold and rainy in Kentucky. I went out to find the mountaintop where Tom had previously sat on a rock that overlooked a beautiful valley. I was singing to him on my way to find this location, and when I got to the area I found a big boulder on top of the cliff on which somebody had painted a five-pointed star, like an X marking the spot. It was where Tom had sat on the cliff, so I sat down.

Tom was already in surgery, and there were four angels protecting the four directions for him. He was on his belly and was unconscious from the anesthesia. The medical team had started the surgery, and I was putting golden Blue Light into the surgical wound when he flatlined.

I moved from the boulder to the top of the mountain so that I could get more energy from the earth. I pulled up everything I could from the earth to help him, and I was breathing for him. Then the monitor showing his heart started to dance again, indicating that life was back.

Spirit told me, "He's okay now; you can go."

I left the mountain and went back to Sidney's. Later that day, she called Tom's wife to find out how he was. Tom's wife told us that she was with him in recovery when he regained consciousness, and he had turned to her and said, "I was with Dan on top of the mountain, and it was beautiful. But why did the son-of-a-bitch move?"

The night before the surgery, when the anesthesiologist was talking to him, Tom had explained that it was important to be careful with the amount of anesthesia because of damage in Tom's lungs. A few weeks after the operation, Tom asked me to come and see him, and explained that the anesthesiologist had given him too much anesthesia, and that was why he had died.

When Tom died the second time, as a result of the overdose of anesthesia, God greeted him and said that he could remain at Home because his work had been completed or he could return to his body again, but it would be without the superhuman powers he had had and his job would be to enjoy his family and teach the priesthood. He decided to return because his grandchildren were not born yet and his wife had not yet been ordained.

He wasn't sure if it was the overdose of anesthesia stopping him from accessing information available to him before his surgery, but he avoided talking about his second death experience because it was overwhelming for him. I felt sorry for him, as he did not have his superhuman abilities anymore; however, he still had phenomenal abilities and wasn't concerned.

A Shift in Ability

After Tom's second death experience, his work was complete and a lot of his abilities had been removed when he returned. I was sad about that, but he was okay with it, and as a result he became more human. At night, he would sometimes go out of his body and leave it cold, but gradually over the years, he became more like the old Tom in the human condition.

In 2007, he made his third and final transition. He used himself up in his service to God and the human condition, just like Edgar Cayce had done. Perhaps this book will be a resource for the many people he served I do not know. He accomplished so much globally and personally, and on so many levels.

Smoking

When I was young I lived in the public housing projects, and we used to collect Coke bottles to sell in order to buy cigarettes. I started smoking when I was 11, but around age 22, when the cigarette packages came out with the surgeon general warnings, I quit.

Someone asked Tom about their personal smoking habits, and if they died from a related illness whether that would be considered suicide. Tom told the person that it depended on one's level of awareness, saying:

"For example, if Chesbro picked up smoking again, it would be considered suicide because of what he knows. However, if someone else who is a habitual smoker has not dealt with spiritual issues, it would not necessarily be deemed a suicide. It would depend on your level of spiritual awareness and enhancement."

So consider the things you can do to balance out your life.

San Francisco, Oakland, and Other Places

Several years ago, there was a major earthquake in San Francisco. At the time, my family and I were sitting in the living room watching TV.

My wife was talking with Tom on the telephone, and suddenly he said: "I have to go. A bridge is collapsing." He said he had work to do, and minutes later, we got the news on TV about San Francisco and the Oakland Bridge. People had died on the bridge, and he was facilitating their transition.

Later, he talked about the people who had died, saying that it was their time to transition because their work was done. Nobody leaves here until their work is done. When you are ready to go Home, you go Home. Your spirit guides help you to make the transition, and nobody fails that; however, if you know your work is done, you can certainly ask for more time on Earth.

There were other earthquakes around the planet, and Tom talked about the natural geophysical function of an earthquake. He also explained the spiritual aspect that moves the human condition ahead, when we willingly show compassion to neighbors with whom we would not normally communicate, such as with victims and their families of these "disasters."

Free Will Choices

When HIV/AIDS appeared here, Tom said that there was no cure, and that there was the possibility that up to two-thirds of the planet could make their transition, either because of that epidemic or another disease. Now it appears that COVID-19, and perhaps additional mutations, might be the other disease.

It was a hard thing to hear, and it is challenging that so many lives are devastated by disease, but guard against taking this as a judgment. People make their own free-will choices and decisions.

What you do with your life during periods of crisis or unfortunate circumstances is what forms character. It is your choice to be compassionate or miserable. It is your choice if your spiritual evolution comes about as the result of a plague.

None of this is about judgment or sin, and it is best that it not ever be thought of as such. We make free-will choices, and have done so for eons. Our choices create the opportunity for situations to occur. One of Tom's choices was to be a Messenger of God so that we would not be annihilated by nuclear disaster.

The Rapture

Tom was asked to talk about the Rapture and the end of the world as prophesied by some religious groups. The Rapture is a theological construct that, according to some, "good" people go to Heaven and the others, the "bad" people, go to Hell.

Tom saw all of the probable futures of the planet and that there was the potential for us to destroy ourselves and the planet through nuclear war, and that was unacceptable. The destruction of the planet through nuclear war could have been considered the Rapture by certain religious groups. However, everyone goes to Paradise; Buddhists, Muslims, Jews, Christians, Hindus, agnostics, atheists—everyone! This is because God loves everyone unconditionally, and there is no Hell. Remember the Law of One: Everything is God, and everything is Good.

Suicide

Frequently, during teaching and in conversations with Tom, people would bring up the topic of suicide, and in all the years he taught about suicide, he never wavered in his comments. Tom said, "There is no sin, but if there were a sin it would be suicide."

Two books were written about Tom Sawyer: *What Tom Sawyer Learned from Dying* and *Tom Sawyer and the Spiritual Whirlwind*, both authored by Sidney Saylor Farr. In both books, the subject of suicide is discussed, but in the second, Tom gives a lot more detail and insight into the devastation that ensues following a suicide. I encourage you to read those sections in both books. I was incredibly moved by the information in *Spiritual Whirlwind*. It is riveting!

Committing suicide is more than just taking yourself out of your life experience. When you remove yourself from the fabric of the Universe, who is there to take your place? You leave a hole in the fabric, and the entire Universe must shift to accommodate your choice (perhaps this is where Chaos Theory originates).

With suicide, it's very challenging for the individual and for the survivors who were in a relationship with that individual. When someone suicides, they are willingly withholding themselves from the Light. This is not about judgment at all. That the person would withhold themself from the Light is their free-will choice; however, the bottom line is that even if someone does take their own life, eventually everyone goes back Home to the Light.

Several of my own friends have committed suicide, at a time when I didn't yet have access to Tom's knowledge and understanding. With any luck, information from Tom shared in this book will provide hope, but ultimately, each of us makes, and is responsible for, our own free-will choices.

Everyone Comes Home

Some folks talk about people going to the dark side and all that that implies. Tom said that there is only God; there is only Good, and there is no judgment about what you choose to do. Tom said that sometimes people choose the dark side, but whether you come Home in the dark or come Home in the Light, everyone comes Home. In a suicide scenario, the time that you choose to withhold yourself from the Light could be vast; however, eventually everyone comes Home. Even if it's the end of time, everyone comes Home. That is, indeed, good news.

A Sentence May Prevent Suicide

I was in Harrisburg, Pennsylvania, doing readings, and one of the people I read for was upset that his girlfriend had committed suicide. He had been offended by a line about suicide in the book *What Tom Sawyer Learned from Dying,* so I told him I would take it up with Tom.

Tom told me that particular sentence was there because the probability existed that someone might use free will to buy the book, read that sentence, and choose to avoid committing suicide. Now, I wonder, how would it be possible to edit such a book, knowing that there could be an important sentence designed specifically for one person?

I took the information back to the grieving and angry man, but he was not appreciative and chose to remain upset. One of the stages in the process of loss and separation is anger. I believe this person was dealing with his process.

The Almighty Takes the Form of a Man

Some time ago, I was made aware of a situation in which someone had committed suicide and a survivor came to talk to me and related that the person who committed suicide had appeared to her, telling her that God had given him permission to take his life.

I called Tom and asked him about this, and he told me that, of course, God would not have said that. He explained that God had taken on the form of the person who had taken their life and given the woman that message to provide her with some solace.

What an incredibly beautiful thing. I was grateful that Tom had shared that with me—that God would love a person so much that He/She would take on the image of a person to provide solace and comfort. It is an extraordinary gesture of Love.

Step Out When You're Done

One evening, Tom and I were talking about people passing over and how that is facilitated.

Tom said, "If you know that your work here is completed, you have a right to lie down and step out of your body."

Some people know when their work is done. They say goodbye to all their family and friends, tie up loose ends, and then step out. If you do this it is not suicide.

Dreams and Your Life Review

Often, when Tom was talking about his death experience, he would talk about his life review.

He said, "In your life review you will reexperience all of your dreams, what they meant, and what your soul was teaching you at night."

As a mammal you have four to seven dreams a night, and perhaps a few during your naps. Even if you can't sleep, if you have a brain you're going to dream. You will encounter every dream you ever had (plus your daydreams) in your life review.

Your dreams constitute an in-house workshop in which your soul is reviewing past or current lives and probably futures. Most dreams are in color, and the colors represent emotions and feelings. When it comes time to evaluate your life, your dreams will help you understand what it is that you learned during your life. Even if you don't remember your dreams, or can hardly recall them, you will still be guided intuitively to a situation where you can gather what you need in your spiritual development.

Spontaneous Combustion

Tom said he was aware of true spontaneous combustion having occurred at least five times as a result of his death experience. He said that each of us has a place located around the heart chakra that contains a spark of the Divine with full memory of being One with God. Each of us can totally recall that in its entirety, and in doing so without any reservation, one could spontaneously combust from the pure, ecstatic joy of it.

As a result, energy would be released, accompanied by a flash of bright white Light that would look blue to the eye, and the smell of a trace of ammonia in the air. Beneath where this happens would be a small amount of what is called gamma ash residue. Some would call the energy the Holy Spirit or the Comforter; scientists would call it neutrinos. We now know that neutrinos travel faster than the speed of Light, which is what Love does. The composition of neutrinos is unconditional Love, God's body.

Tom shared with us that both Melchizedek and the Master Jesus returned Home through spontaneous combustion. The trick is to be complete in all that you came here to do.

Prayer over Coffee

One afternoon, my former wife and I were meeting Tom for lunch at a local diner. Upon arrival, I spotted him sitting in a corner in a business suit, apparently praying over a cup of coffee.

We joined him, and I asked: "What's with the praying over your coffee? Is it that bad? Why are you in a business suit?"

He answered: "I had a previous appointment that I had to be dressed for. In a parallel Universe, I would have died today of a heart attack, so that's why I was sitting here in prayer."

The men in Tom's family all passed over at an early age from heart problems. His talking about a parallel Universe and the probability of his dying in that Universe was the first time that I had ever heard him express anything about such concepts.

Everything Is Mathematical

When Tom had his death experience and merged with Total Knowledge, everything was in a mathematical formula. It struck horror in me to hear him say that everything was a mathematical formula, because I am . . . well . . . not so good at math. I thought I wouldn't understand it. He said that I would probably see art, because I am an artist. If you are a musician, you may experience everything as music; if you are an artist, you may experience everything in colors. There are billions of musical compositions and colors in the Light.

Corralled Horses

Tom told us of a plane crash in which military people and scientists had been passengers and passed over. He said that the unfortunate part of this event was that the plane had crashed in a field where horses were corralled, that in the wild, horses would not have corralled themselves and had perished. The people on the plane had spiritually contracted to make their transition together, but the horses could not escape, and that was the unfortunate part.

It was interesting to witness the audience response to what Tom said. They were somewhat shocked that Tom did not consider the deaths of the people to be the unfortunate part of this crash.

Tom said, "It was a free-will choice on the part of those on the plane that they were going to go Home together when they passed over, but the horses could not escape."

Defending Your Life

Several years ago there was a motion picture written by Albert Brooks called *Defending Your Life*. The movie is about what happens during a life review. Tom and I and our wives were watching the movie at Tom's house, and Tom said that not everybody needs imagery in their life review, although this movie was about two people who required imagery. In Paradise, for example, a person can eat whatever they like and not get fat.

It was interesting to watch the movie and hear Tom comment, "Somebody knows something!" He was referring to the information portrayed in the movie; that there is truth in it.

In the movie, Albert Brooks is having his life review and staying in a hotel where he finds breath mints left on his pillow. Meryl Streep is also in the film, and she has chocolates left on her pillow.

Brooks asks her, "Why are you getting chocolates when I'm getting breath mints?" She replies, "Because I deserve it!"

Paradise and Heaven

Tom talked to us many times about what happens when you pass over. You will have a guardian Angel that takes you to a place called Paradise. The lights in Paradise are called Heaven. Paradise is a dimension where imagery is continued as a way of relating to reality; however, depending on your spiritual development, you may bypass the world of imagery and go directly into the Light.

A Short Life

Oftentimes in our meetings with Tom, folks would ask "what if" questions. Someone asked him a question about infant death. He said that whether you have come to live for a few minutes or a hundred years, you will have the opportunity to fulfill your contract. It doesn't matter if someone dies from sudden infant death syndrome (SIDS), for they are no less fortunate than someone who dies at 89 years of age.

I would imagine that for an infant, if there is a life review, it is going to be a very short one, but it could include the planning for that life, who the parents are that were chosen, and what gender, race, blessings, or infirmities were chosen to be manifest. There are no accidents, and prior to your birth all those things (and more) are predetermined by you, using your free will. If you only live a few seconds, you planned that also.

You gain a very different perspective if you understand that a life planned for a few moments was chosen by that entity and is no less valid or valuable than one chosen to last 89 years. If you understand this, then an infant's death may not be viewed as an unfortunate event, for it is always a free will choice.

Tom would always say, "Look at the big picture." It may not be immediately possible to see the bigger picture, though, if you're in grief over the loss of a loved one.

No Premature Death

Sometimes, we wonder why certain things happen as a person's life draws to a close. Tom said, "How you are born is how you will die." It is all about balance.

For example, if someone lives a life of rigid independence and won't allow anyone to give them anything, they could potentially live their last days totally at the mercy of others to feed, clean, and/or clothe them. When there is a natural death, there is the fulfillment of that life. No one gets out until their work is done. When your body dies, you graduate and go Home.

Anwar Sadat

Part of the plan for the New Age is that millions of people born on the Earth plane of their own free will will choose to have a near-death experience (NDE) in order to change their perspective and attitudes, thereby serving as a catalyst for world change. Included in this group will be world leaders, who will help make the change into the Age of Aquarius.

One of the world leaders who had an NDE was the former President of Egypt, Anwar Sadat. (Some other major leaders in the Middle East also had NDE transformations.) As a result of his NDE, Sadat's perspective and attitude became more tolerant, compassionate, and open-minded; however, this made him more intolerable to his enemies. All this was prior to the Gulf War, and was part of a strategy to avoid nuclear conflict. Tom talked about Sadat as being a key player in this strategy because of his NDE, but many people don't like or want change. It was most likely

Sadat's more open-minded attitude about Israel that prompted fundamentalists to assassinate him and try to take conditions in Egypt back to when they were less open and compassionate.

Divorce

Oftentimes during Our Pal Joey conversations, people would bring up more mundane questions, and one was about divorce. Tom would say that some people need to divorce; that sometimes people get along better when they are not living in the same house.

Tom also said that once you have been married and had sexual relations, there is a bond that divorce doesn't break; that once you are married, you are married forever in this life. Sometimes after divorce we experience that through dreams. A former spouse can take on the role of teacher in your dreams, for example, as they had done in the relationship.

Tom also said that divorce is hard on children, no matter how young or old they are. What's interesting to note is that when both parties make their transitions, they are no longer married, as at death you do part. If you are passing over and want to see your loved one, they may appear in your life review or tunnel experience, but there is no marriage in Paradise—there is no reason for it. You can get divorced legally on this side of the veil and physically separate, even though divorce doesn't exist until you make your transition. Marriage is spiritual, biochemical, and emotional, and lasts until both parties pass over.

I'm Done—I'm Going Home Soon

On several occasions, Tom talked about what would happen toward the end of his life. One time, after the Christmas holidays, he called several of us together to talk about this. He told us that he would have thinning hair and many other physical changes because he would consume his physical body energy in service to the human condition, just as Edgar Cayce had done. He also told us that some friends would reject him. He told us what was going to happen far enough in advance so that we would be prepared. It was the completion of his life and his mission, and it would be his time to graduate and return to the Source. As in the movie *Star Wars*, when Obi-Wan Kenobi was struck down by Darth Vader, Tom would then be available everywhere, in all time and space.

We'll Be in Communication

Early one afternoon I went back to the farm for something I needed for the Priesthood Conference. When I opened the door the phone rang.

It was Tom, who asked: "What are you doing home? They're looking for you at the conference."

I told him that I had just come home to get something for the conference and then I said, "Tom, while I've got you on the phone, when you finally pass over and stay there, am I still going to be hearing from you?"

He said, "Yes, of course, we will be in communication."

I said that I thought that was so, but that I wanted to hear it in my physical ear.

Prior to, and since his passing, I have seen him on several occasions in dreamtime. Once he was in clown makeup, and his message was to "Keep it light." In another dream, he was piloting a ferryboat full of people, helping them to "cross the river," as in helping them to make their transition. The last communication I had with him was in a dream. We were sitting across from each other at a table, and he said to me that the children involved in the Occupy movement would soon be met with violence. It was a short time later that this occurred in many places.

He taught me years before (not in dreams) that the world would evolve into a place of egalitarianism, or equality, among all sentient beings; that we would have a peaceable kingdom here, but that we would always have to deal with greed and ego. I realize that the Arab Spring and the Occupy movement are only two indicators of evolving global affairs signaling the end of patriarchy and the beginning of equality in this Age of Aquarius.

Don't Worship Me

Periodically, Tom would talk about what he wanted to happen to his body after he died. He was concerned that he would be turned into an icon and a temple built in his memory or honor, and he did not want that. He said, "Wrap me in a sheet, take me out in the woods, and leave me there to feed the porcupines."

Legally, you can't do that, but he would often joke about it. His real plan was to be cremated and his ashes spread on Lake Ontario. Once in a while, he would talk about his death and emphasize that it was not to be a sad thing. Worship God, but not one of God's messengers.

Healing

Love Balming (Love Bombing)

People frequently asked Tom about facilitating healing, and whether he had suggestions for doing that.

He said to avoid telling the sick anything of a negative nature. Avoid telling them your woes or any sad stories, what's wrong with this or that, or what's nasty in the news.

Instead, use lots of humor, tell them jokes, and even bring a joke book with you—in other words, make them laugh. In addition, be sure to touch them, to establish a physical connection, and if you are inclined, use the laying on of hands to do that. All the while, open your heart and hold the intention of beaming Love at them. Prayer also plays a big part in healing.

His term for all of these actions collectively was "love balming." When you visit the sick, love-balm them and get them to laugh. These acts will pick up their energy if they are meant to heal.

The Cat and the Cancer

This story is about Ed. Ed was a client of mine, and I used to do readings for him. I told him in a reading about a cat that would come to be his pet. He was not really interested in having a pet, nor a cat, but then somebody gave him one. He was coming down the stairs one day, and the cat got in his way, so he tripped and fell on his side. When he went to the doctor for the pain in his ribs, they found out that he had cancer.

Sometime after that, we spoke on the phone, and he asked me if he could meet Tom Sawyer. He said, "I've heard you speak a lot about him, and I would like to meet him."

I told him that I would try to make the connection to Tom for him, and during the course of our conversation, he mentioned that he lived on a cul-de-sac.

I was going away on business that weekend, so I called Tom and asked if he would go see Ed. Tom answered, "Oh yes, he lives on a cul-de-sac, and he keeps asking for God's help, but he won't let me in."

Ed died some time later, and to my knowledge he and Tom never physically met.

A Man Called Stan

Stan had been in Vietnam and sprayed with Agent Orange. Later, he developed cancerous tumors throughout his body. While I was teaching in the Carolinas, I was asked to go see Stan in the hospital, and he was very gaunt. We had a lengthy conversation, and before I left I kissed him on the check and said, "You know, you could still be well." I remembered feeling somewhat guilty about having said that, given that he seemed so close to the end of his life.

When I returned to Rochester, I met with Tom and explained my feelings, and Tom said, "Don't worry, I've checked out the tumors, and he will be okay." I later realized that Tom had taken all of Stan's tumors into his own body, allowing Stan to leave the hospital cancer-free.

When Stan first came out of the hospital, he was in remission, and I went down to talk to him. We were on our way to an Egyptian exhibit, and while driving, he told me how he had liked to write when he was in high school.

He said that one night he had had a dream about a person by the name of Sam Clemmons, author of the well-known book, *The Adventures of Tom Sawyer*. In the dream, there was an African American who brought a rocking chair onto his porch for Sam Clemmons and then Stan and Sam (aka Mark Twain) were rocking together and Sam said to Stan: "You know, you really should be a writer. You really write well."

So I said to Stan, "Gosh, you know someone by the name of Tom Sawyer who brought you back from the grave, and you could write a story for Readers Digest about the most incredible man you've ever met. Don't you get it? Tom Sawyer—Mark Twain?"

Stan lived two or three years after that, and in that time, he and his wife had a baby boy. But Stan went back to his old patterns and got sick again.

Before he died, he called Tom and thanked him for the extra years he had had and for being able to see his son born. But he never wrote anything in this time.

Young Man in the Hospital

Tom heard of a young man in the Midwest who was getting ready to make his transition, and he went to meet him. The young man's sister was trying to see her brother before he died, so Tom asked God if he could live another day or two. God said, "Okay." The young man lived long enough for his sister to get to see him one last time and then he passed.

Years later, I was working in Michigan, and a woman said to me, "I heard you talking about Tom Sawyer today." She said she had met him many years ago, and continued, "I was trying to get to the hospital to see my brother before he died, and I met Tom Sawyer at my brother's bedside."

I was incredibly moved and told her that Tom had facilitated her seeing her brother. What a beautiful, loving gesture that Tom was able to provide for the sister and brother, asking God to intercede on the sister's behalf so that she could see her brother before he went Home.

Patty's Hearing Loss

My youngest daughter, Patty, has hearing loss in one ear and was taken by my wife, Carol, to see Filipino healers who were visiting the community. Patty was young and very fearful that they would hurt her in some way and didn't want to go back for another treatment. The person hosting the healers called my wife and demanded that she bring Patty back, which resulted in Carol feeling guilty about not doing so. Carol spoke with Tom about it, and Tom talked to Patty. He told her: "I love you just the way you are, and if you don't want to go, I still love you just the way you are."

Heal Yourself in the Morning

Tom gave us a good suggestion for healing ourselves. He suggested that upon waking in the morning, before getting out of bed, give yourself a healing, Reiki, prayers, positive affirmations, or something to create your self-healing, and then start your day.

Earth Happenings

The Great Pyramid and the Earth

I've done four ceremonies in the Great Pyramid in Egypt. Afterward, there was always a sprinkling of mist or rain above the pyramid and a small earthquake on the opposite side of the planet.

Many years ago, I was in a bookstore at an airport and saw a book entitled *Krakatoa*. Spirit said that I ought to read this book, and I thought, if it is for sale on the other side of the airport, then I'll buy it. I went to the other side of the airport, and it was for sale.

Toward the end of the book, there was a lot of information and research concerning Edgar Cayce. Cayce said that the last time there was great tectonic activity on the planet was 10,500 years ago. Apparently, the ocean's bottom has a zebra pattern that can be read and tells the earth's history, and the pivotal point for all tectonic plates for the planet is under the Great Pyramid. Long ago, the ancient priests would do ceremonies to bring in the Light, and it would go to the core of the earth and cause seismic activity. It was exciting to see the scientific data corresponding with what had occurred during our visits there.

My sister, Doris, who is also a near-death experiencer (she died when her daughter was born), was shown by Jesus that the Blue Light comes from beyond the Bear Constellation, beyond the North Star. It shines through two angles. One is the Christ Light, which was used by the priests in the Great Pyramid and is still used for ordination ceremonies today.

The Great Pyramid's four sides represent the four elements and the fixed signs of the zodiac. The fifth point is the apex of the pyramid—the Light of God. The Great Pyramid is an incredible living thing that can energize Earth.

In the ceremony in the Great Pyramid, when we invoked the Light it was from the Melchizedek teachings of long ago. These teachings later became the source for the Kaballah. In the ceremony we used a Melchizedek meditation incorporating earth, water, fire, air, and Spirit.

In all the years I have gone there, I have not been in the other two pyramids. I had a dream one night that I was in the King's Chamber, also known as the Hall of Initiation. Some stones were moved and a hallway was revealed. I was looking down the hallway, and in front of all the rooms off the hallway, there were jinns—in this case, thought forms of protection. Tom taught us that the ancient priests sealed the rooms of the pyramid because ignorance was coming into the world. They put a deadly fungus powder in the rooms before sealing them. If somebody without full knowledge violated those rooms, they would quickly die from this poison. Much later, this was interpreted as the Pharaoh's Curse.

The Photon Belt

At a luncheon at our friend's house, the subject of three days of darkness came up. Someone asked Tom if it was true that Earth was to undergo a great transformation as a result of passing through a photon belt. Tom made it clear that this was not going to happen. He said that there would be no three days of darkness and that we had nothing to fear.

He said to me: "Dan, if this were true, wouldn't I have told you? Somebody imagined it and promoted it, but it is not real."

Shifting the Poles

Several years ago, there was a lot of concern about the possibility of a magnetic north/south polar reversal.

Tom said: "Dan, if there was a complete pole shift the way people are talking, the human race would be destroyed. It would cause tremendous disturbance and destruction. We would all die. The earth wobbles around the sun, and so there can be a little distortion in the magnetic field, but if the poles were to completely reverse it would cause great devastation. That's not going to happen."

High-Water Marks

When Tom's first book was released, he was invited to be on the *Good Morning America* show in New York City. Afterward, he went walking in the city and noticed that there were high-water markers, 20–40 feet up from the street on the sides of the buildings.

He said, "Gee, I don't remember there having been a flood here." Then he realized that what he was seeing was a probable future. With global warming, it's probable that the oceans will rise to that height and most of New York City will be inundated with rising tides.

The Genesee River

Quite some time ago, I had a dream about living at the farm and the house being surrounded by water; it wasn't possible to get to work unless I used a boat to reach my car. Tom said that, at some point in the future, the Genesee River would probably change its course, and in so doing would return to where it had originally run a long time ago—through my back-yard. There is a creek back there right now, but it could be the riverbed in the future, as rivers do change course. I guess that gives me an opportunity to get rich selling live bait and/or having river-front property.

China and Capitalism

Oftentimes, Tom would talk about political issues. His insights about political matters came from his death experience. He said that China was going to be an economic contender soon, and that capitalism would change the face of China.

The Five Resident Saints

Tom taught that there are five resident saints on the planet at all times. They do not meet, but they do know of each other. They would not neces-sarily be deemed saints by the Roman Catholic Church but are considered saints by the Creator. Most people will never know them, nor even know of them. They are committed to world service, and each oversees an area of responsibility on the planet. When one of them passes over, someone else takes up their position; since Tom's passing in 2007, I'm sure that another saint has stepped in to take his place as one of the five. One day, while flying to Virginia, I asked him telepathically about this.

He let me know that, at that time, one of the saints was a woman living near New Zealand.

Lovely Lessons

The Lesson of Free Will

When God imagined the creation of souls and a Universe in which we can express ourselves, souls were given free will. What I learned from Tom is that free will and God are equal in power, allowing you the ability to imagine separation from God. If you can imagine it, you can have it.

In truth, you can never be separate from God; however, you have imagination and free will, so you can "pretend" that you are or that there is no God. Likewise, you can have "Hell on Earth" as a creation, if you so choose—God will not violate your free will. Therefore, imagine what you would like, and using your free will, take steps toward creating it (you do this all the time anyway).

If you take one step forward, God will facilitate your desire or dream. In that way we are all godlike, because we can create. We can think about things and mull them over and have emotions about them. Matter comes from thought, and we allow the Universe to bring things to us by using our free will. Understand that there are no coincidences nor accidents when something is created in your life. You are the cause of all of your effects.

For example, when people worry, they are creating the very thing they are worried about because of the energy they are putting into it. The gift of free will is generally not promoted by churches, and to say that you love yourself is not generally accepted, but unless you love yourself as God does, unconditionally, not much can happen. If we love ourselves as God does, we will come to the point of creating as God does and will be co-creators with God.

Unconditional Love

One of the things Tom taught was Unconditional Love. Many evenings he came to teach in a beauty parlor. He would bring a valise filled with papers and fumble through them, probably assessing the issues for the group that evening, then he talked to us for hours and hours.

One night, he said that there are only two beings in the entire Universe who can give you Unconditional Love: God is one, and you are the other; therefore, since 50 percent of the battle is won, why are you holding out? In the womb you can hear your mother's voice, and it becomes a part of your identity or ego after you're born. As you grow and mature people tell you things, many of which are negative, so most of us don't love ourselves. Many of us don't like ourselves as a result of our life's experiences and what we have been told, but God loves us unconditionally. It doesn't matter to God what you think about yourself; God already loves you, and you are the only other one who can love yourself unconditionally as God does. It behooves you to do that.

God is a storehouse of benevolence and loves to be generous, but if you will not allow yourself to be loved you do not receive, and in so doing, you are not allowing the flow of energy to complete itself. God would like you to receive the things you desire, and you might receive it through another person, even a former enemy. To love yourself unconditionally is to allow yourself to receive. Many of you are great givers, but not so good at receiving. Giving and receiving need to be equally balanced. So ask permission to give, and be willing to receive.

Dr. Masaru Emoto and his work with water crystals demonstrated that the words Love and Gratitude have a powerful effect in forming beautiful water crystals. Love is what you give to others, while gratitude is in the receiving. That is the give and take. It is every bit as important to receive as it is to give, so allow others to love you back.

Be mindful that these are all about free will—both the receiving and the giving. If you continue to give someone without their consent, they may eventually come to resent that, and someday cross the street to avoid you. The solution is in asking permission to give before you give. What matters is that there is an energy exchange. Go back to basic English class and look at the difference between the words "can" and "may." The word "can" implies having a capability; the word "may" implies having permission. So one would ask, "May I describe this or teach you that?"

Where two or more are gathered, the energy can flow. For example, you can ask, "May I offer you a Qigong session." If they say no, fine, walk away. Allow them to be. Spiritually, it is important to ask permission to give. When Tom announced that there are only two who can love you unconditionally, I realized that God does not require anything for me to be worthy of His Love. He/She has no conditions. In other words, I don't have to meet any requirements for God to love me. There are no conditions upon which you receive God's Love. Everybody is perfect just the way they are. Remember, none of God's creations are junk.

The Shroud of Turin

Someone asked Tom whether the Shroud of Turin was an authentic relic. As a result of being in Total Knowledge, Tom answered yes.

The linen is herringbone woven from materials available at that time, and the image was not embedded on the linen itself but on the filaments of the linen. After his death, Jesus transformed his physical body to a Light body. That was the resurrection. There is an energy released from this transformation. The resurrection experience is similar to a supernova, and a brilliant white Light (which would look blue to your eyes) would emanate from it. There would also be a trace scent of ammonia in the air, and the filaments on the shroud linen would hold the resulting gamma ash residue. The mystics called it "The Comforter" or "The Holy Spirit"; the scientists called it neutrinos.

Tom said, "Isn't it wonderful to think of all the scientists and investigators holding the material that was wrapped around the body of Christ/God?"

Tell Us about Jesus

A group of us gathered at Tom's house around Christmastime one year, and someone asked Tom to tell us the true story of Jesus. He said no, and explained that the scriptures already contained enough of a combination of myth and truth to suffice. He also said, "You could not grasp the whole truth of the mission of Jesus."

Whenever he would say something like that it would seem like an affront at first, but I came to understand and accept that he always had good reason for what he said. They asked him about virgin birth, and he told us that Mariam's (Mary's) mother had not known a man when she was conceived, and Mariam had also not known a man when Jesus was conceived.

The Farmer in His Field

At a Christmas gathering, Tom told us about a farmer in Bethlehem who loved the land and loved to farm. However, he had developed severe arthritis in his hands and could no longer do what he loved. One night, the farmer was standing in his field when the Magi and their entourage came looking for where the mystical child Jesus had been born. The old farmer knew, and he raised his withered finger and pointed the way to the grotto where Mariam, Joseph, and the Christ Child were. That is how the Wise Men were able to find baby Jesus.

Sometimes, simply pointing the way is the fulfillment of your life purpose. Only someone such as Tom, who had Total Knowledge as a result of his death experience, could have known and related this little bit of history.

John the Baptist

Tom was talking one night about John the Baptist, a cousin of Jesus. John's father was Zachariah, a priest in the temple, and his mother was Elizabeth, Mariam's cousin. Elizabeth was an Essene, but Zachariah was not. Because Elizabeth was Zachariah's wife, any male child she bore would typically have been brought into the priesthood to serve in the temple, but because John was not a Levite, this created a terrible conflict for the temple priests.

When Mariam (Mary) became pregnant, she was told to visit her cousin Elizabeth, who was pregnant with John. When John was born, as a way of resolving the conflict, Zachariah was killed in the holy temple, with his hands on the altar. Elizabeth then fled with her infant son to Egypt. Later, of course, Joseph, Mariam, and Jesus also fled to Egypt. So Jesus and John were raised together in Egypt.

Tom had a great sense of humor. He said: "You know, when John the Baptist used to baptize people, he held them under the water a long time. Ask God if John the Baptist nearly drowned everyone."

So we were left to wonder whether that induced a near-death experience, and whether those John baptized "saw the Light," so to speak.

Teaching on Bell Rock

Tom accompanied us to Sedona, Arizona, to visit the energy vortexes on several occasions. One afternoon, it was a pleasure for me to see him standing on the flat red surface of Bell Rock, with students gathered around him. It reminded me of Jesus teaching the Sermon on the Mount, and it felt so good.

Wearing Robes

I come out of a Baptist tradition where we wore black robes in service, and I was always comfortable being a minister in a robe. On one of our trips to Egypt, we had gotten some galabeya robes. Tom, seeing me in my blue galabeya as I was about to perform a ceremony, said, "Gee, I didn't realize that we're still wearing robes." I haven't worn one since. It is a very freeing thing that we don't separate ourselves from the people we serve.

Can I Acquire Those Abilities?

Several years ago, someone asked Tom, "How could I get to have the psychic abilities that Dan Chesbro has?"

He replied: "It is very simple. Go out in the woods, and sit for three days and three nights. Don't bring a book or a radio or any distractions. Just go sit and listen. When you come out of the woods after three days and three nights, you will have developed a sensitivity you did not have before, and that way, you can continue to develop your spiritual gifts."

There Is No Anti-Christ

One day I went over to Tom's house, and we had a private talk. I was sharing with him that I had had a dream when I was very young about a person in the Middle East who would possess the powers of an anti-Christ, a person who was very handsome and charismatic and would draw thousands of people to him.

Tom replied: "How can there be an anti-Christ? If there is only God and only Good, how can there be an anti-God? There are those who play a certain role in history, but there is no evil, no sin. These things have been created by us and the human condition."

Alone = Al One = All One

At one point in our relationship, I got angry with Tom and shut him out. He said that there were very few people on the planet he could connect with. He said that he felt lonely when I was frustrated with him and not communicating with him. I vowed that day that no matter what I chose to feel, he would always have an open door to my consciousness and my heart.

He said to me on this occasion: "Whatever happens to you, happens to me. We can never ultimately be separated… You know, Dan, I am an actor—I am playing the part of Tom Sawyer."

Help on the Path

There was a local gentleman who owned a car dealership. We would have fun talking about spirituality over coffee, and I used to do psychic readings for him. Our relationship developed into an ongoing friendship.

Tom said to me: "You know, he is here to help you. You need a good car to do your work."

That same dealer helped me get cars for my children as well. He was an amazing person, for the Blessed Mother had appeared to him when he was a child, and he anonymously did many things to help people in the local community. For example, if he found out that you needed surgery and didn't have the financial means, he would contact his lawyer and arrange for everything, anonymously, to be done for your benefit.

The last time I saw him was after 9/11. He had moved out west, but to my surprise he was at the dealership the day the service department told me that I should think about getting a new car. We talked, and he picked out my 626 Mazda. I trusted him.

Now I miss him, and who knows if our paths will cross again? But it's wonderful to know that a special car dealer was put on my path to help me to get my job done.

The Edgar Cayce Connection

Tom said to me, "You do realize that there is a connection between you and I and Edgar Cayce?"

I responded, "Yes, I know."

Edgar was an incredibly clear and true psychic channel. He gave himself in service to the human condition during the Second World War, and in so doing depleted his life force. Edgar Cayce died January 3, 1945.

Who's Hot?

At the beginning of every year, Tom and I would get together and he would ask, "Who's hot this year?"

He would be referring to the current "stars" of the New Age movement. I would share with him who was current, and he would say, "Well, in two years they will be a distant memory," and he was always right.

He said, "You, on the other hand, are authentic. You will be here after all the others are gone."

I used to ask him what I should say when people asked me about these new "stars" in the metaphysical Universe. After all, some folks didn't particularly want to hear what I had to say; they preferred to listen to one of the "stars."

Tom replied that whatever they teach, as long as it does no harm and it helps folks get through the day, then it's okay.

Runway 22

The number 22 is considered a master number, so it is important to the Order of Melchizedek. When Tom worked for the municipality of Greece, New York, one of his jobs was working at the airport in Rochester. One day he talked about Runway 22, which he helped to build.

I think it is serendipitous that he was responsible for building Runway 22 at the Rochester airport.

Total Knowledge

Tom's first death experience was a blending with God and, therefore, Total Knowledge. All past, present, and probable futures were conveyed.

Total Knowledge = Compassion;
Compassion = Unconditional Love;
and Unconditional Love = God.

I Desire to Know

You do not need Total Knowledge to be a compassionate person. It was incredible to ask Tom questions such as, "With Total Knowledge, do you have intimate knowledge of every being?"

Tom answered yes, there was not a single person whom he did not know intimately and personally, including details of their lives.

Total Knowledge is also Akasha, the storehouse of all experience. Tom would say, "I desire to know," and then he would be given access to Total Knowledge of any subject. That's a great expression, and one we all need to use: I desire to know.

Judge Not

One night, we asked Tom, "Is it appropriate to be in the judgment seat?"

He replied: "In order for you to judge someone or some situation, you would have to possess Total Knowledge of that person or event. It is not possible in the human condition for you to hold Total Knowledge in your physical brain, and therefore you would misjudge. You would have to know all their past lives for you to be a proper and good judge. This is not possible. Therefore, judge not, as you will fall short, and the judgment you dispense will eventually come back to you. God, who is the only entity that could do this, does not. There is no judgment. There is no sin. There is no evil."

A Mass for Hitler

Tom used the experience of Hitler as a teaching tool for forgiveness and compassion. He said he had gone to several Roman Catholic churches and asked them to say a mass for Adolf Hitler. Only one agreed to do it.

Tom was asked why he'd done that, and he said that Hitler was also a creation of God, playing the role of a villain, and because he committed suicide he had gone into the black void. Tom said that a mass may help Hitler to reach self-realization. The upshot is this: a Catholic priest said mass for Adolf Hitler because Tom Sawyer requested it.

The Jesus Tapes

When Tom came back from his first death experience he had access to Total Knowledge, including knowledge concerning the life and times of Jesus Christ. The Near-Death Hotel at the University of Connecticut was the beginning of the creation of the International Association of Near-Death Studies (IANDS). Tom was asked to speak about the life and times of Jesus Christ. Those sessions were all audiotaped and the tapes given to one of the organizers, who stored them in a shoebox on a shelf. The shoebox and tapes disappeared and have never been found. Some of us endeavored to find them, but like Arthur's quest for the Holy Grail, we never did.

He Never Read the Book

Several years ago, I had a friend who was HIV positive and struggling with the passing of his partner a few months before. I told him about Tom Sawyer, and he said he was interested in reading the book about him, so I gave it to him. He wanted to meet Tom, but it just wasn't happening, and it made my friend very angry. What I learned from Tom later was that although my friend had been given the book, he had never read it and really wasn't interested in doing so. Oftentimes, things happen in people's lives, and they have an opportunity to move forward spiritually but are not interested. It could have been helpful to my friend, given what he was dealing with, but he just wasn't interested.

A Hug from Oprah

Tom had been on the Oprah Winfrey Show and told his death story. At some point, we were discussing hugs and hugging and who gives good hugs. (If you ever got a hug from Tom, you would feel him doing light acupressure on your back.) Tom said that one of the best hugs he had ever got from anyone on this planet was from Oprah Winfrey.

The Bright Little Boy

We were having a priesthood conference at Geneseo College, and a young couple there had recently had a baby boy and asked me to baptize him. I had gone home and met up with Tom on the way back to the college.

Tom noticed a rainbow in the sky and said that this boy had the potential of being another Albert Einstein (and of course, Tom would be able to recognize that). At the age of five, the boy made the choice to become a priest in the Order of Melchizedek. That young man is now in his 20s, and it will be interesting to see what free-will choices he makes. Even with Albert Einstein, there were failures with math, ridicule, and so on. This young man has also experienced challenges.

Tom Meets Albert Einstein

When Tom had his first death experience and gained access to Total Knowledge, he became intimately aware of the life of Albert Einstein. He also became aware that Einstein and his scientific colleagues, such as Niels Bohr and Max Planck, were all very distressed that the work they had done was being used to develop nuclear weapons.

Tom experienced such intimate knowledge of this group of scientists during his death experience that when he came back, he thought that he could just get together with them over a cup of coffee. He was disappointed to find out that they were not in the physical anymore.

Later on, Tom sent a message to Albert's surviving sister that Albert was at peace because the threat of nuclear warfare was no longer a reality. Tom implied that Albert Einstein was a very spiritually enlightened being.

Make the Invitation

Tom was sharing with us about his spiritual enhancement, and he said that after his first death experience he could go into any church, temple, synagogue, or place of worship and find God there. Tom said that when Roman Catholic priests invoke God's presence for communion at mass, the Spirit of God is there but that the priests would not necessarily have any idea of what they had invoked. Tom said that when there is any ritual and God is invited, God comes.

The Best Snow Plower

Tom occasionally would talk about his work as a heavy equipment operator. He worked in asphalt and road repair and fixing water main breaks. Rochester winters can bring large snowfalls, and part of his job was to drive a snowplow for the city. He used to say, "I am the best snow plower in the northeast." Some people thought it was arrogant on his part to say that, but if he said that he was the best, then he was the best. That's not arrogance; it's simply the truth.

Medications

Tom was telling us about some of the side effects that our teenagers would probably experience at the onset of this New Age. Because of the nature of the hormonal changes in their bodies, it would be difficult for some to adapt to the extreme shift of energies. Tom discussed the use of certain prescription drugs on young people and said that one of the eventual side effects might be that they would turn violent. At that time, there had not been any shootings in schools or shopping malls, so we wondered where he was coming from with such a statement. Part of this is also the increasing stress in the human experience from a variety of sources. He was aware of all this as a probable future from his death experience. Unfortunately, now we are witnessing it.

Your Right to Demand

People often talked to Tom about personal difficulties in their lives. He said to them, "You know, you have a right to demand of God that these things cease."

He was sharing an interesting concept—that you have a right to demand that it stop. God will then do an intercession or bring one or more other people into your life to help. Similarly, in prayer, it will serve you better to avoid asking for what you want, and instead, command it to take place. After all, you are an aspect of the Almighty, a function of the Light, a god or goddess in training. So command what you want and then express your gratitude as if your command has already been produced.

Prayer and Meditation

Several years ago, I had a friend who was a habitual user of recreational drugs and was experiencing shortness of memory. Tom said that if that person decided to live a life of prayer and deep meditation, they would build brain cells. When you are focusing on a connection to God and give up drugs, you can build brain cells and go on to live a good and balanced life. Even though some scientists say it's not possible to grow new brain cells, it is.

Jesus and Buddha

One evening, we were talking about the lives of Jesus and Buddha, and Tom had some wonderful insight from his death experience.

He said: "What I learned in Total Knowledge was that Jesus was born enlightened, and that Buddha, departing from his father's palace, saw death and depravity, which drove him to sit under the Bodhi tree and attain enlightenment by demanding it."

Millions of people follow both Buddha and Jesus. The role model is that you can be born into enlightenment or become enlightened through a path of dedication and prayer. It's your choice.

Soul Evolution

One of the questions somebody asked Tom was, "Does the soul evolve?"

He replied: "No. The soul is an aspect of God."

As personalities, we can evolve. The free-will choices we make in this lifetime affect our next incarnation. Your highest self could be attaining the quality of soul, which is perfection. In terms of one lifetime to another, you are dealing with subjects or conditions that facilitate the growth of your ego personality and your role as a co-creator, but your soul would not experience that angst. Your soul is the point of expertise that gives you information—in your dreams, for example; as an aspect of God, it does not evolve. Likewise, this talk of there being "old souls" and "young souls" is inaccurate. Being an aspect of God, we are all "old souls"; we have all been here since the beginning.

The Fourth Dimension Is Truth

One night we were discussing different levels of reality, and what Tom said was interesting.

"If you are in the fourth dimension, which is like being in a Plexiglas cube, and you have an insight that came from that dimension, which is Truth, then that is Truth throughout the entire Universe."

So, for example, in a fourth-dimensional meditation, if you receive the information that God is Love, then that is Truth throughout the entire Universe.

Change Your Attitude

In life experience, we always have an attitude about things, ourselves, our communities, and so forth. It is sort of like a belief system. Tom said that if you change your attitude you can shift a galaxy; that is, a change of attitude about anything can change everything. It behooves us to love ourselves more—love ourselves unconditionally—as it produces the availability to change our incarnation in the next life as we are beginning to exist in the next dimension. If you want a better life in this life and in your next life, change your attitude, especially about Love and Compassion. That will result in good all around.

Antigravity Vehicles

In the late 1970s, we were dealing with the first energy crisis and a shortage of gasoline accompanied by inflated gasoline prices. And here we are again, in the new millennium, with high gas prices and vehicles that don't get great mileage. Tom said many years ago that, in the future, we will have antigravity vehicles that work like magnets that repel each other. It reminded me of *Star Wars* and the land rovers that could hover. I'm looking forward to that one, and I'm surprised that someone hasn't come up with it yet to help us toward the greening of the planet.

Lower Back Pain

Several times, when Tom was teaching, he said, "Don't be surprised if some of you have lower back pain in the next week." This was the result of the energy being shared and how it affected people's spines. The pain was due to the kundalini rising and working toward their enlightenment.

There was a time back in the 1980s, during the Harmonic Convergence, when there was a lot of energy coming to the planet and people's heart chakras were expanding. Many folks mistakenly thought they were having heart attacks. The more you practice Love, Service, Compassion, and Justice, the more the evolution of self takes place.

An Old Carpenter's Tool

Tom was, ironically in a sense, a carpenter, and a good one. Periodically, I would think about him and the role he played as a carpenter. He would talk about a tool called an adze, which was used long ago for planing. An old Tibetan carpenter gave him one.

Tom had work that needed to be done in his attic, and before he died, he posted what was needed on a beam up there so that the person who did the work would have his instructions. He was a very good carpenter. I know of one other spiritual teacher who was also a carpenter.

Montreal Melchizedek

A few years ago, we went to the Cathedral of Notre Dame in Montreal. The altar is surrounded by niches lit with blue lights and filled with one or more statues of Biblical characters. To the left of the altar is a statue of Melchizedek. He stands next to a stone altar, with a loaf of bread in one hand and a cup in the other (this statue is frequently mistaken for Jesus).

After we visited the cathedral, we went to lunch. I had been expressing some personal challenges, and Tom leaned toward me and said, "I don't remember Melchizedek ever whining or complaining about his work."

Take Two Steps Back

Tom was talking to us about ways to handle an argument with somebody. He said it would be far better to take two steps backward and then turn and walk away than just walk away. Taking these two steps constitutes a symbolic disconnect and dissociation and is less offensive to the other person than just walking away.

I Didn't Ask for That

Tom and I were traveling out of Virginia and flying back to Rochester after a conference, and on the way to the plane, out of nowhere, a man showed up and took Tom's valise to carry for him.

We got on the plane, and I asked Tom, "What was that all about?"

He said: "I didn't ask for that. The Universe just decided that I needed a little help."

When the plane landed, and we got off, there was a flurry of monarch butterflies that flew all around him, welcoming and greeting him.

Caring for Your Pet and Your Pet Caring for You

Those of you who are animal lovers will appreciate this. A friend of ours had a dog that was very elderly and had gotten to the physical condition to be euthanized.

Tom's comment to her was: "When you have a pet and you domesticate it, you are responsible for its life and death. Although a cat can never be totally domesticated, a dog can. A dog is so attached to its master that it will live beyond what it normally would, so it's your responsibility to be sure that when it's time, you take it to be euthanized. Cats, on the other hand, living in the wild, will go under a tree and leave."

Tom offered to take our friend's elderly dog to be euthanized. But the woman said, "No, it's my responsibility."

On the morning of the day that she was going to put him to sleep, she told the dog what she was going to do that afternoon. The dog had not been going out for quite some time, but after she went to work a relative living in the house let him out.

The dog went out into the road and was immediately killed by a passing vehicle. The dog knew what was happening and decided its owner shouldn't go through having to take it to the vet.

The Fellow Who Threw the Bike

One night at one of our many gatherings at the beauty parlor, Tom told us a story about one of the few times that he had cried prior to his death experience.

In his youth, Tom had been infatuated with a young girl and frequently rode his bike several miles to visit her; when she moved quite far away, he still rode his bike to see her. Eventually, he got married—but not to the girl with whom he had been infatuated.

As a young man, he enjoyed biking so much that he developed himself into an Olympic-caliber bicyclist. He continued with his biking career and qualified for the Olympics in Mexico City in 1968.

The bike he was taking was shipped by plane; however, there was a young fellow who was on his first day at his job at the airport and wanted to impress his co-workers. He threw Tom's bike into the cargo bin and bent a wheel. Tom didn't discover the damage until he was at the track, and once the bike arrives at the track neither the Olympian nor their bike can leave, not even for repairs.

Tom realized his only choice would be to race with a bike that had a bent wheel. After years of discipline, training, and developing himself into an Olympic bicyclist, it was over for him—over before it even began. That was when Tom lay down and cried. It was very moving to hear him tell this story. He was not angry with the fellow; he was disappointed with the outcome and wept in frustration.

Now consider what happens to that young fellow when he dies and has his life review. He will see everything in his life, including the day he threw the bike, and he will know the bike was damaged because of his ego. He will see/feel Tom's anguish and experience his tearful devastation. He will fully realize all that it meant to take that opportunity away from another person. There is no judgment about what he did, but he will be made to know the full result of his choice. How often do we do things in life unaware of the ramifications of our free-will choices? It's not about judgment, but about being a creator and what you create, and therefore, what you are responsible for.

The shortest sentence in the entire New Testament describes what Jesus did after a loss: "Jesus wept." (John 11:35) Tom wept as a result of his experience. In time, when that fellow passes over and has his life review, he may get to meet Tom and bring that experience into balance.

A Simple Stopper

We were asking Tom about the effects of marijuana. He said a lot depended on the use pattern. He told us about a young man who was a habitual user of marijuana, which resulted in the usual lackadaisical attitude about things. This person worked at an airport and part of his job was to check oil levels in airplanes.

There was a little rubber stopper that had to be replaced every time the check was complete. The man just chucked it over his shoulder, because he had a predilection for letting things go, but this eventually resulted in a plane crash.

He didn't realize that throwing away the rubber stopper would cause a malfunction and people and horses would be killed. He didn't think about that outcome because of his lackadaisical attitude, but in his life review, he will relive everything and understand all the ramifications of it.

How many and what kinds of things in life do we discard because we don't think it matters? If you are hired to do a job, you do it, and take an extra few seconds to consider the possible outcomes of your choices. Still, God will not judge.

The Doubt Factor

Even though Tom had been with God and directly experienced Total Knowledge, he still doubted some things. It seems that doubt is an integral part of the human condition.

There were two incidences I know of where Tom verified information he had received during his death experience. One was returning to one of the places in his life review. When he beat the old man who had staggered out in front of his truck, he had the simultaneous awareness that several blocks away there were paint cans on top of a building. Many years later, he went back and found that the paint cans were still on top of the building, exactly as they were in his awareness during his life review.

The other situation was on Chokpuri Hill, Tibet, where he wept upon seeing the crack in the Holy Mountain, for he had seen it during his death experience. He doubted certain things and wanted to relieve his doubts by verifying them.

It seems to be important for humans to know that there is a backup way to ascertain what we doubt. Tom felt that he had somehow doubted what God had said until he saw and felt it for himself. God had told him that the New Age of Aquarius would start with a series of earthquakes and volcanoes, and that one of the earthquakes would split the Holy Mountain, so seeing it was proof of God's revelations to him.

Consider what your life could be like if you stopped doubting all that God is providing.

Communion, Perfume, and Aftershave

In the first several years of the priesthood, we had priesthood gatherings in Geneseo, New York. We had a communion service and placed a loaf of unleavened bread and seedless grapes on a plate, and people served themselves.

Tom brought to our attention that since the service took place in the morning, a lot of attendees had just shaved, showered, and put on their colognes and perfumes and all those scents were being transferred from their hands into the bread. He suggested cubing the bread so that it wouldn't accumulate perfume and aftershave. It's not a good idea to provide a ritual that is problematic for some people.

The theme for this evolving New Age is equality for all; therefore, we must endeavor to be sensitive, compassionate, and as accommodating as possible. Ideally, everyone feels valued and included. I myself wasn't being very sensitive, because there were Jewish people attending, and one came forward to tell me that they were uncomfortable with the communion service and talk of Jesus.

I eventually stopped serving communion in order to avoid having people with other religious proclivities feel excluded. I realized that I needed to expand my awareness and be more inclusive. Melchizedek served bread and wine, and we were sharing that symbolism, but I still needed to be sensitive and compassionate. In truth, communion happens in your heart and mind; it doesn't have to happen with bread and wine.

Supraluminal Telecommunication

When Tom told the story of his death, he coined the phrase "supraluminal telecommunication." He used this phrase in reference to those precognitive communications, or Love Gestures, that were coming to him, and that that energy was supraluminal in terms of the speed it traveled.

He also used supraluminal telecommunication in reference to a high degree of spiritual communication. Tom had realized when he was going through the tunnel after his death that he was going faster than the speed of light. It has also been discovered that neutrinos travel faster than the speed of light. The composition of neutrinos is the Unconditional Love of God. Know that Love travels faster than the speed of light.

Warmed-Over Alice Bailey

Oftentimes, Tom would talk about the New Age and New Age teachers, and he would say that there really was not much new being brought forward by new teachers, that it was mostly warmed-over Alice Bailey teachings.

Alice Bailey, Madame Blavatsky, Rudolph Steiner, and Edgar Cayce were forerunners of the New Age. In their time, they were on the cutting edge of ideas for the new consciousness of the Age of Aquarius, but their teachings got a cold reception from most people of their day.

Today, near-death experiencers provide more of a secure footing in the New Age.

Tempting the Almighty

I don't remember when this event happened, but Tom told me the story about his having tempted God. He became curious about what he could or could not do to his body as a result of his death experience. Thinking that he was truly blessed, he took a knitting needle and was going to push it through his arm.

As soon as he touched the needle to his arm, an unseen energy threw him across the room and into the wall. He was almost knocked unconscious. He said that he learned a very important thing from this experience: Don't tempt God, and/or don't mess with the Energy.

I believe this event had to do with his ego and violating his temple—who/what he had become as a result of his death. The Energy that picked him up and threw him was quite powerful, so obviously it's not a good idea to mess with the Boss. Always remember, "Thou shalt not tempt the Lord, thy God." (Deuteronomy 6:16)

The Last Talk

One day, while exercising at my local gym, a woman asked me if I was Dan Chesbro. I replied yes, and she introduced herself. She had had a near-death experience and was a Catholic, and she wanted to talk to me.

We chatted for some time, and on another day, she came over to the farm for lunch and we continued our conversation. She related to me that when she woke up from her NDE, she was completely cured from lupus.

I gave the woman copies of Tom's videoed talks, so that she could share them at future IANDS meetings. She had met Tom at an IANDS meeting, when he gave a talk shortly before he died. It was one of the last talks he gave before his final transition. Even with his last breath, practically, he was doing his work to share his knowledge.

Kateri and the Five True Saints

Several years ago, Tom championed a Mohawk and Algonquin woman called Kateri Tekakwitha born in 1656. She was often referred to as the Lily of the Mohawks, and the Roman Catholic Church was in counsel as to whether to canonize her. She was declared Venerable by Pope Pius XII on January 3, 1943; beatified by Pope John Paul II on June 30, 1980; and canonized by Pope Benedict XVI on October 21, 2012. She is the first Native American to be sainted.

Tom was very enamored of that. I'm not sure why except that she had lived near a part of New York State where he was raised.

Tom shared with us that there are five saints on the planet all the time, and that they are "true saints." It is their job to keep the planet safe—theirs is the energy that keeps the planet together. He shared with me that at one point, there were four men and one woman. They all know of each other, but it is not necessary for them to meet. That realm of sainthood is different from the Roman Catholic Church sainthood. They are contemporary and are true saints.

Endings

What Time Is It?

We were doing a conference and needed a photograph of Tom. I had an old Polaroid camera and hadn't used it in a long time. We went to his home to take his picture. When we arrived, he was singing in the shower. When he came out to greet us, he had his blue shirt on. He asked his wife if she had bought the single-edged razor blade he had asked her to buy. When I took the first picture, I needed a razor blade to clear out the camera trap as the picture had jammed.

Following that, Tom's wife asked him, "Tom, what time is it?"

Tom threw his head back and laughed as he responded, "If you were asking Jesus Christ this question, He would say that this is the fourth time that time is coming to an end."

Tom later explained to me that there was a Big Bang that initiated the creation of the Universe. We are approaching the fourth time that the expansion is coming to an end. It takes billions of years for the Universe to expand, but only millions for it to contract in what is called "The Big Crunch."

Tom said that we would not always be carbon-based units as we are now and would become more spiritual beings.

Love Gestures

In 1987, and again in 1988, there were several Love Gestures given by God to Earth for the purpose of assisting the human condition. Pure Love is given to us from God as Pure Knowledge and Inspiration, but because we have free will we can choose to reject it.

There was a time when a critical mass of events and probable futures came together that could have resulted in the annihilation of the human race, and a decision needed to be made by God concerning Creation. The question was whether to eliminate the human condition before we destroyed the planet or bombard us with Unconditional Love in the thought that, with free will, we would take advantage of this Love and rectify conditions on the planet and with each other. So the Almighty sent massive doses of Unconditional Love energy through Light from quasars in outer space, while avatars and angels became incarnate in order to facilitate the conditions for change.

We did not have a nuclear war thanks to interventions by Tom Sawyer. We still struggle, however, with whether we as individuals and as a collective will choose to love ourselves. Love Gestures can come through pure Light, inspired books, poems, paintings, people teaching through their example, and so forth; all are ways to open to unconditional self-love. And these Love Gestures will not be curtailed, even up to the end of time (if there is an end), because there is a never-ending supply of probable futures. Always believe in the availability of miracles, divine intrusions, and angels, because those are always options. Wake up, get busy, and choose compassion.

As we go forward in time, new world leaders will be spiritual leaders or they won't be elected to positions of power. That is also a Love Gesture. Our goal is to eliminate all suffering for all sentient beings. Love yourself unconditionally as God does, and do at least one thing each day to bring this outcome into reality.

Tom said, "We are living in a period of Grace," and also, "We will have a peaceable Kingdom."

The Great White Brotherhood

When I was coming into my ordination work, I became aware of the concept of the Great White Brotherhood. The only issue with using that terminology in these times is that it could be misconstrued as racist and/or sexist. "White" refers to the blending of all colors. The concept of brotherhood was brought in as an attempt to bring the human family together, but now we are at the point where we are moving into egalitarianism.

The Great White Brotherhood's commitment is to help the human condition, and part of the Order of Melchizedek priesthood is involved in that. "Children of the Light" may be a more suitable term. We are all in this situation together, and there is a Matrix of Energy that permeates everything. Love yourself, love your neighbor, and love God; they're all the same thing.

This seems to be about the struggle locally and internationally of who will allow or not allow working, playing, and loving together without discrimination or impedance. Peace (at all levels) is what it is all about.

As things evolve and time moves along, the individuals going into politics in this New Age will have to demonstrate the qualities of true spirituality or they will not get elected. This is not about a religion at all, but about spirituality.

Spirituality has no fear—it is about experiencing the Oneness of all things. Take a lesson from John Lennon's song Imagine: "Imagine there's no countries / It isn't hard to do / Nothing to kill or die for / And no religion, too / Imagine all the people, living life in peace." In John Lennon's time, people continued to talk about brotherhood.

Everything begins with thought and becomes form. Everything is acceptable unto God. Tom was a messenger from God who came to help us realize the possibility for a peaceable kingdom, and begin making it happen; to have the opportunity for self-realization and self-Buddhahood and fully realize that "When two or more are gathered, there I am."

According to some physicists there is no time, only the present. When you go off the planet, how can you tell what time it is? We have imagined boundaries, where there are none. This is the time when those separations get recognized for the illusions they are. Be mindful of the Law of One: There is only God; there is only Good. We have the responsibility of gods and goddesses in training, for that is what we are, and what we create is our responsibility. We really need to be compassionate.

The Great White Brotherhood was created long ago to bring these ideas forward. Many of the instructions of Melchizedek were provided to bring these goals to fruition. Ignorance is not bliss. Love yourself as God does. Love your neighbor as yourself, and love your house plants, the beings that swim in the waters, the four-legged, the winged ones, and so forth. We will work this through. It is not the end of the world. It starts all over again.

The Paramedic's Experience

What follows is a shortened version of things that happened to a paramedic who accompanied Tom to the hospice for his final care. She did not know Tom, nor know of him, prior to assisting him in getting to the hospice. She stated that she never had any experiences that anyone could label as being outside the range of what all of us would call "normal." She had worked as an EMT for 16 years and been present when many people "graduated," but of course, that was expected in her profession.

Keep in mind that Tom had specifically advised many of his friends that after his death, they should not expect to hear anything more from him—he clearly had other plans and would not be in touch.

The day the paramedic assisted Tom's transport started in an unusual manner. She had the freedom to take an extra shift, and the supervisor asked her to do just that. By her reckoning, neither of these things ever happened to her! Once she was settled in the rig with Tom and a junior EMT, she decided to take over the patient's care—another thing that was unusual, as typically the junior person takes the lead, while the senior EMT supervises as necessary. To this day, she says that she doesn't know why she did this; she just felt she was "supposed to."

The ride to the hospice was otherwise uneventful, and Tom told them about his life and how proud he was of his wife and children. When they got there, another odd thing happened: four hospice nurses accompanied them into his room. Usually only one nurse goes along, and sometimes a tech as well.

Routinely, as soon as everything is in order, the paramedics leave. Usually, this paramedic had little connection to a patient and, as professional self-protection, "turns off" whatever connection is there as soon as she leaves the room. But she said goodbye and touched his shoulder for a long time, then his leg, and finally, his foot, and realized that she wanted to stay. Apparently it showed, because out in the hall one of the hospice nurses asked if she was okay. Strange!

In the days that followed, she found herself thinking about Tom and telling several people about him (omitting his name, of course). She wondered why this dying old man was taking up so much space in her head. She even thought of visiting him, but remembered that he had said absolutely no visitors. None of these things were at all typical for her, which was not usual.

Then she read his obituary in the paper and was shocked by it, as if she somehow thought that he wasn't really going to die. Throughout that week she thought of him many, many times.

One morning, a little over a week after his passing, she felt his presence very strongly, as though he was right there next to her in the room. She also gradually came to understand that she was having his feelings and thoughts. At first she panicked and believed she was losing her mind, but slowly she came to understand Tom, his sense of humor, his teasing, his intent, and what he wanted her to do. In addition, she gradually learned to distinguish what was him from what was her. Within a few days, she was speaking to him directly (out loud), and he was responding by giving her unmistakable feelings and images.

None of this was easy for her. She struggled with it and often thought she was going insane. Consequently, she devised "tests" for herself to see if she was imagining it all, but every one of them left her convinced that it was all real. For example, in one test, she put a rock in each hand and proclaimed that left indicated yes and right indicated no. She stated that if all this is real, and this is really you (Tom), then give me a sign. The left rock flew out of her hand.

Tom provided information for her to write for his wife and children. In the process, he let her know that death does not stop Love, and you continue to love after you graduate.

So she wrote it all down, and at Tom's insistence, delivered it to Elaine, his wife, along with a book he wanted her to have. She and Elaine wound up talking on several occasions, and she found that what she and most of us might think was weird was taken as typical by Elaine, who was quite used to such things.

It was only afterward that the paramedic discovered many of Tom's friends, the books written about him, people who knew him, and people who would help her develop her own rapidly blossoming psychic gifts and abilities. Today, she is actively serving the Light and furthering Tom's work in her own way.

In one of her conversations with Tom, he let her know this: "It's time to get my friends moving. It's time to continue spreading my message of Love. There are enough people that if they continue the work, it will make a difference." And addressing "his people" directly, he said: "You've had enough of a break; it's time to get cracking. Each of you has something to contribute in your own way, so get going!"

New Beginning

The last several years of Tom's physical life, he had problems with his lungs and possibly brain cancer. Tom, like Edgar Cayce, had consumed his life force in service to the human condition.

A nurse who had met Tom at one of his talks years earlier happened to work at the hospice where he died. She was scheduled to work on the day after he died and arrived to hear her colleagues talking about this man who had come in the night before, carrying his own oxygen and announcing that he was going to make his transition that night. He knew his work was done; he had fulfilled his contract.

As you may recall, Tom was born on the 9th month, on the 9th day, the 9th hour, the 9th minute, the 9th second, into infinity, which is the numerological value of a High Teacher and Redeemer. When they assigned Tom to a room in the hospice, it was Room 9. He was admitted on the 27th of April and made his transition on April 28, 2007, which was his wife's birthday.

Numerologically, when you reduce 28, it becomes 1, which indicates New Beginnings.

Tom Sawyer

9th September 1945 – 28th April 2007

A Chronology of Tom Sawyer

1945	(Sept. 9)	Birth. Mother has him baptized "Tom Sawyer," reason(s) unknown.

1945   (Sept. 9)   Birth. Mother has him baptized "Tom Sawyer," reason(s) unknown.

1951   Begins attending Henry Lomb School No. 20, Rochester, New York.

Works 3–4 weeks on a dairy farm during several summers.

1959   Elaine Powers meets Tom and tells her sister she's going to marry him.

1960–1965   Has paper route.

Becomes a skilled bicyclist.

Meets and trains with Vince Maxwell, speed skater, who races bicycles to stay in shape during the summer.

Wins city and county championships in novice class speed skating.

Meets Mike Carnahan and helps coordinate and promote the Classic Bike Race at Lake Canandaiqua for the Windmere Cup until 1978.

Registers with the Selective Service.

1964	(June)	Graduates from Benjamin Franklin High School, Rochester, New York.
		Lettered in track and swimming.
		Becomes an apprentice carpenter.
1966		Dates Elaine Powers and falls in love with her.
1967	(Aug.)	Selective Services classified 1A (Available for Military Service) with a low number. Calls Selective Services to ask why he hasn't been drafted. (Tom was never drafted; reason(s) unknown.)
	(Aug. 12)	Tom Sawyer and Elaine Powers are married.
1968		Employed at Alhart Hardware and Appliances; works evenings in gas station.
		Later drives garbage trucks.
		Employed by Rochester Department of Public Works, eventually operating many forms of heavy equipment.
		Olympic Trials.
		Bicycle is damaged so he cannot compete in Summer Olympics.
	(Dec. 28)	Tom and Elaine's first son is born.
1973	(Dec.)	Ends bicycle racing career.
1974		Tom and Elaine's second son is born.
1977	(Jan. 30)	Tom and Elaine buy their first home.
1978	(May 23)	First death experience at 6:41 p.m.
		Sends 25-minute tape of death experience to Dr. Kenneth Ring, University of Connecticut.
		Participates in a documentary entitled *Prophetic Voices*, which becomes a 25-minute educational film and wins documentary award at the North American Nurses Education Association Film Festival.

1979   Paints the formula for matter waves on the top and sides of a junk van and slowly tows it past the University of Rochester and the Laser Research Lab and the Research Center on Quantum Physics, where the Omega Project is housed. Staff crowds the windows writing on notepads.

Shares information of a precognition involving a nuclear detonation in the Middle East at the Near-Death Hotel (the residence of Dr. Kenneth Ring)

Creates a list with the title "1981, as Seen from 1,000 Feet Above."

Appears in a commercial film, *Prophetic Voices*.

Appears on 20/20, *ABC News Magazine* with Steve Fox; *ABC News* at 6 pm and 10 pm; Channel 13, Rochester, New York; and CBS *Night Watch* with Dr. Bruce Grayson.

1982   Appearances at University of Connecticut, (and continual participation in ongoing NDE research) Storrs, CT.

Speaks at Monroe Community College.

Appears at Yale University Symposium with Drs. Raymond Moody and Kenneth Ring.

Begins talking of Earth changes happening from the mid-1980s to 2000.

Lectures at the Spiritual Frontiers Fellowship Conferences.

1983   Talks at the Monroe Community College.

Featured in newspaper and magazine stories by Steve Straight: "Einstein and the NDE" and "Straight's Unprovable Tunnel Theory: Vital Signs".

Talks at the International Association for Near-Death Studies (IANDS).

1983 (Feb.) Appears with Rev. Dan Chesbro on TV show *Open Door*.

Appears on *Afternoon Exchange* with Charles Flynn, Ph.D., Columbus.

Featured on *The Last Word*, ABC Nightly News.

Featured on *Morning Break* with Don Alhart with live call-ins.

Lectures at the Association for Research and Enlightenment with Dr. Raymond Moody and Milton Friedman.

Lecture at the Spiritual Frontiers Fellowship Conferences.

(July) Arthur Sawyer, Tom's father, passes away in Rome, New York.

(Oct.) Has a precognition of the crash of a L-1011 plane at Dallas–Fort Worth Airport, TX, on August 2, 1985.

1984 Appearances at the University of Miami; Conferences for Medical Professionals, Oxford, Ohio.

Talks at Monroe Community College.

Talks at various Spiritual Frontiers Fellowship Conferences.

Talked about in IANDS journal *Anabiosis*, Vol. 4, #2 (Fall 1984).

Talked about in *National Inquirer* article: "Near-Death Experiences Improve Peoples' Lives."

1985   Featured in "Death" by Ray Finger, *The News Leader.*

In "Beyond and Back" by Kimberly Wynn, *Democrat and Chronicle Upstate Magazine.*

Appears at the Kubler-Ross Symposium, International Association for Near-Death Studies (IANDS), University of Connecticut.

Lectures at the First Lutheran Church, Teen Lectures, Rochester, New York.

1986   Talks at Corning Community College, Corning, New York.

Talks at Symposium on Death and Dying, School of Nursing, University of Connecticut.

Talks at Stuben County Social Services Nursing Program, Bath, New York.

Featured in "Back from the Great Beyond" by Ansi Vallens, *Women's World.*

Guest on the *Oprah Winfrey Show.*

Lectures at The Crystal Voyage, Summer Sunday Workshop.

Talks at Trinity Episcopal Church, Rochester, New York.

1987   Enrolled in Rev. Dan Chesbro's workshop, Teach Them to Fly.

Lectures at Spiritual Frontiers Fellowship Conferences and Order of Melchizedek Priesthood Gathering.

(July 1)   Meets Sidney Saylor Farr in Lynchburg, Virginia, who will author *What Tom Sawyer Learned from Dying* and *Tom Sawyer & The Spiritual Whirlwind.*

1988		Appears at Northern Kentucky University, St. Luke's Hospital, and the National Pastoral Council, Covington, Kentucky.
	(Oct. 16)	Guest on the *Phil Donahue Show*. Prepared to disclose information about the Middle East precognition, but is approached by two military men who convince Tom it is not necessary to bring up the subject.

Talks at the Berea College Sunday Night Chapel Speakers, discussion group afterward, then lectures at Spiritual Frontiers Fellowship.

Lectures at Visions of Tomorrow Conference, Geneseo, New York.

Lectures at Visions of Tomorrow Conference, Roanoke, Virginia.

Order of Melchizedek Priesthood Gathering, Geneseo, New York.

Pilgrim Church, Boston, Massachusetts.
Zurn Lecture Hall, Villa Maria College, Erie, Pennsylvania.

Begins conversations with Rev. Dan Chesbro for anchoring the Blue Light around Earth in proximity to 33 degrees north latitude.

1989   (Jan)   Sidney Saylor Farr commits to writing *What Tom Sawyer Learned from Dying*.

Tom and Elaine's second son fractures arm and has multiple lacerations in auto accident. Grandpa Gene Powers prays with laying on of hands, and Melchizedek priests do distant healing.

Features in "Back from Beyond" by Karen Krenis in *The Times Union*.

Appears on *The Geraldo Show.*

Featured on *Unsolved Mysteries.*

(May 4)   The Blue Light is anchored in Hawaii.

(July)   Series of interviews by Carol Chesbro ("Tom Sawyer of America"); many are available on You-Tube.

Lectures at Visions of Tomorrow Conference, Geneseo, New York.

Lectures at Order of Melchizedek Gathering, Geneseo, New York.

1990   Guest on *Good Morning America.*

(Jan.)   Lectures at Berea College's Saturday Morning Dialogue on Campus.

(Jan. 29)   Second death experience during back surgery. "Volunteers" to remain on the planet; receives information to teach the Priesthood of Melchizedek; slowly begins to lose many of his extraordinary abilities.

Lectures at Visions of Tomorrow Conference, Geneseo, New York.

Lectures at Order of Melchizedek Gathering, Geneseo, New York.

1991   Lectures at Visions of Tomorrow Conference, Geneseo, New York.

Lectures at Order of Melchizedek Gathering, Geneseo, New York.

(Sep. 15)   Ordained into The Order of Melchizedek by Rev. Dan Chesbro.

First trip to work with groups and individuals in India, Tibet, and Egypt.

1991	(Nov. 22)	Completes anchoring of the Blue Light in Egypt with Rev. Dan Chesbro and 133 Melchizedek priests.
1992		Lectures at Visions of Tomorrow Conference, Geneseo, New York.
		Lectures at Order of Melchizedek Gathering, Geneseo, New York.
1994	(Aug.)	Audio recording of *Tom Sawyer and the Spiritual Whirlwind* by Sidney Saylor Farr.
1995		Second trip to Tibet with a group of 27; audience with the Dalai Lama.
1996	(Apr.)	In tornado in Berea, Kentucky.
2007	(Apr. 28)	Third and final death experience—graduation—on Elaine's birthday.

Recommended Reading

Bettelheim, Bruno. *The Uses of Enchantment.* New York: Vintage Books, 1977.

Chesbro, Daniel and Erickson, James B. *The Gospel of Thomas.* Forres: Findhorn Press, 2012.
——. *The Order of Melchizedek: Love, Willing Service & Fulfillment.* Forres: Findhorn Press, 2010.

Emoto, Masaru. *The Hidden Messages in Water.* New York: Atria Books, 2004.

Farr, Sidney Saylor. *Edgar Cayce's Story of the Bible.* Virginia Beach: A.R.E. Press, 2012.
——. *Tom Sawyer and the Spiritual Whirlwind.* Berea: Omchamois Publishing, LLC, 2000.
——. *What Tom Sawyer Learned from Dying.* Norfolk: Hampton Roads, 1993.

Moody, Raymond A. *God is Bigger than th e Bible.* Sarasota: Life After Life Institute, 2021.
——. *Life after Life.* New York: HarperCollins, 1975.

Ring, Kenneth, Ph.D. *Lessons from the Light.* Needham: Moment Point Press, 2006.
——. *Heading Toward Omega.* New York: Harper Perennial, 1985.

Sanderfur, Glenn. *Lives of the Master.* Virginia Beach: A.R.E. Press, 1971.

About the Authors

Rev. Daniel Chesbro is an American Baptist minister who trained at Andover Newton Theological School, Crozer Seminary, and Colgate Divinity School. He served congregations in Boston, Philadelphia, and Rochester & Webster, New York. He was the host of the television show *The Open Door* and founded a modern-day School for the Prophets to offer the world community access to ancient and present truths.

Dan combines sensitive intuitive abilities with a ministerial background, psychological training, metaphysical knowledge, and a wonderful sense of humor to teach, guide, and enhance the lives of those he encounters. He lives in Conesus, New York.

For more information on the Order of Melchizedek
see the Sanctuary of the Beloved at:

http://goldenlionmedia.com/sotb

Rev. James B. Erickson was raised in a family that saw to it that he received a healthy amount of religious education. Over time, he became aware of what he perceived as incongruities, irrationalities, and ultimately unanswered questions in that education. This precipitated a thirst for knowledge, a search for answers, and a quest for Truth that continues to this day.

In the pursuit of those things, he became a therapist, studied historical and sacred writings, developed his psychic abilities, discovered his gift of clairsentience, and became a lifelong learner.

He was ordained into the Order of Melchizedek 30 years ago and actively supports its mission and goals. James lives in Minneapolis, Minnesota.

FINDHORN PRESS

Life-Changing Books

Learn more about us and our books at
www.findhornpress.com

For information on the Findhorn Foundation:
www.findhorn.org